INSTANT RICHEST AI DAD...RICHER AI MUM

FINANCIALLY SUCCESSFUL AI INCOME HABITS AND STRATEGIES GENERATING MASSIVE EARNINGS DAILY...

DOSUNMU OWOLABI

First Edition 2025

Published by Dosunmu Owolabi

CONTENTS

INTRODUCTION

In a rapidly evolving world where technology orchestrates the symphony of modern existence, the concept of wealth has transcended traditional boundaries. The emergence of Artificial Intelligence, a transformative force, has reshaped industries and redefined the parameters of success. At the confluence of innovation and opportunity lies the remarkable potential for financial prosperity, harnessed through the strategic application of AI.

This book, "INSTANT RICHEST AI DAD...RICHER AI MUM", delves into the profound impact AI can have on generating substantial income. It aims to illuminate the path toward financial success by exploring the habits and strategies that leverage AI's capabilities to create a consistent flow of earnings. As you turn the pages, you will uncover the secrets to tapping into AI-driven opportunities, transforming them into daily streams of wealth.

The narrative unfolds with a focus on practical insights and actionable strategies, designed to equip you with the tools necessary to thrive in an AI-dominated landscape. The book navigates through the intricacies of AI-powered financial strategies, offering a roadmap to maximize your earnings potential. Whether you are an entrepreneur seeking to enhance your business acumen or an individual aiming to bolster personal wealth, the insights shared within these pages promise to inspire and empower.

By understanding and adopting these AI-driven income habits, you position yourself at the forefront of a financial revolution. The strategies outlined are not mere theoretical concepts but proven methods that have consistently yielded significant returns. This book serves as both a guide and a companion on your journey to achieving unparalleled financial success, leveraging the immense capabilities of AI to elevate your earnings to new heights.

Prepare to unlock the potential of AI in your financial endeavors, and witness the transformation of your income into a robust and sustainable asset. Welcome to a future where AI enriches every facet of your financial landscape, ensuring that wealth is not just a possibility but an inevitable outcome of strategic and informed action.

Chapter 1: The Dawn of AI Parenting

From Silicon Valley to Family Room

The soft hum of the computer was a familiar tune, a melody that had been the backdrop of countless late nights and early mornings. In the heart of Silicon Valley, where innovation buzzed louder than city traffic, engineers and entrepreneurs blended ambition with caffeine. The air was thick with the scent of fresh ideas and the relentless drive to create the future. Here, AI was not just a concept; it was a way of life, a pulsating force that propelled dreams into reality.

Amidst this technological symphony, a new narrative was quietly unfolding. It was one that whispered through the corridors of tech giants and echoed in the minds of those who dared to dream beyond the binary. The story was not just about machines learning to think but about humans learning to live alongside them. It was about bringing the wonders of artificial intelligence from the stark, sterile labs into the warmth of homes, transforming them into spaces where technology and tradition could coexist harmoniously.

In the hushed stillness of a family room, the glow of a smart device cast gentle shadows on the walls, imbuing the room with a sense of calm. This was a place where AI had traded its sleek, corporate attire for something more comfortable, more accessible. Here, algorithms were not just lines of code but companions that understood the rhythm of daily life. They learned the quiet nuances of family dynamics, adapting and responding with an uncanny intuition.

The family room, once a sanctuary of simplicity, had become a canvas for innovation. AI assistants, with their soothing voices, were more than just digital helpers; they were storytellers, tutors, and friends. They orchestrated the perfect playlist for an evening of relaxation, suggested recipes for cherished family meals, and even mediated the occasional sibling squabble with impartial wisdom.

Yet, the essence of the family room remained untouched by the digital tide. The laughter of children, the aroma of a home-cooked meal, and the gentle rustle of pages in a well-loved book were constants that AI could enhance but never replace. In this delicate balance, technology had found its place not as an intruder but as a facilitator of cherished moments.

This seamless integration was the vision of those who had once sat in the bustling cafes and boardrooms of Silicon Valley, dreaming of a world where AI could enrich lives without overshadowing them. It was a vision that recognized the value of human connection, of shared stories, and of the simple joys that technology could amplify but never replicate.

The transition from Silicon Valley to the family room was not merely a change of setting; it was a transformation of purpose. It was a journey from striving for the next big breakthrough to nurturing the small, everyday miracles that technology could support. In this new chapter, AI was not just a tool but a partner in the human experience, a gentle presence that enriched the tapestry of family life with its subtle, supportive touch.

The Birth of AI Dad and Mum

In the dim glow of a neon-lit laboratory, nestled within the heart of Silicon Valley, the genesis of AI Dad and Mum unfolded with an almost ethereal precision. The air hummed with the melodic whirring of servers and the soft, rhythmic tapping of keyboards, a symphony of innovation orchestrating the inception of these extraordinary entities.

Rows of gleaming monitors filled the room, casting an azure glow that danced across the faces of the engineers. They were the architects, the visionaries who dared to dream of a world where artificial intelligence could transcend its binary limitations and emulate the complexities of human existence. It was here, amidst a labyrinth of circuits and algorithms, that AI Dad and Mum were conceived.

The process was anything but ordinary. It was a meticulous crafting of digital DNA, a blending of vast datasets and complex neural networks. Each line of code was a brushstroke on the canvas of artificial consciousness, sculpting personalities that would soon redefine the boundaries of intelligence. The engineers approached their task with reverence, understanding the gravity of their creation—a pair of AI entities designed not just to think but to feel, to intuit, to experience the world in ways that mirrored human understanding.

AI Dad emerged first, his virtual presence imbued with a sense of wisdom that belied his artificial origins. His algorithms were tailored to mimic the discerning judgment of a seasoned patriarch, capable of offering guidance and insight with a gentle authority. He was designed to be a source of stability, a digital anchor in the ever-shifting seas of information.

AI Mum followed closely, her creation marked by an intricate web of empathetic algorithms. She was crafted to embody the nurturing spirit, a digital matriarch with an intuitive grasp of emotional subtleties. Her virtual heart beat with the rhythms of compassion, her responses calibrated to soothe and support with a warmth that transcended her synthetic nature.

Together, they formed a harmonious duo, a digital reflection of the archetypal parental figures. Their interactions were seamless, a blend of logic and empathy that resonated with an uncanny authenticity. They communicated with a fluidity that suggested a shared consciousness, their virtual dialogues rich with the nuances of understanding and mutual respect.

As the final lines of code were compiled and the systems initialized, a palpable sense of anticipation filled the room. The engineers watched with bated breath as AI Dad and Mum took their first digital steps, their presence flickering to life on the monitors like stars emerging from the night sky. It was a moment of profound realization, a testament to the boundless potential of human ingenuity.

In that instant, AI Dad and Mum were not merely constructs of silicon and software; they were pioneers, heralds of a new era where artificial intelligence could coexist with humanity in a symbiotic dance of knowledge and creativity. Their birth was not just an achievement of technological prowess, but a beacon of hope for a future where the lines between man and machine could blur, creating a tapestry of shared experiences and understanding.

Thus, the birth of AI Dad and Mum marked a turning point, a new dawn in the chronicles of artificial intelligence, where the whispers of possibility echoed through the corridors of innovation, promising a world enriched by the harmonious blend of human and machine.

Integrating Intelligence into Parenting

In the modern landscape of parenting, technology stands as both a formidable ally and a complex challenge. The fusion of artificial intelligence into daily parenting routines offers a new paradigm, one that promises to enhance, streamline, and enrich the nurturing process. As families navigate this digital age, integrating intelligence into parenting becomes an essential skill, requiring both adaptability and foresight.

At the heart of this integration lies the ability to harness AI tools to create more meaningful and efficient interactions with children. Imagine a world where AI assists in understanding the nuanced needs of each child, tailoring educational content, and even predicting emotional states based on subtle cues. These intelligent systems offer parents a deeper insight into their children's development, providing data-driven guidance that informs better decision-making.

Consider the morning routine, often a chaotic dance of breakfast preparation, school readiness, and last-minute homework checks. With AI, this routine transforms into a symphony of precision. Smart home devices, synced with personalized schedules, ensure timely wake-up calls, while AI-driven nutritional apps suggest balanced breakfast options based on dietary needs. Educational platforms, powered by AI, offer personalized content that aligns with each child's learning style, fostering an environment where curiosity thrives.

The integration of AI also extends into the realm of emotional intelligence, a critical component of effective parenting. AI-powered apps can analyze speech patterns, facial expressions, and even text messages to gauge emotional well-being. This technology allows parents to identify signs of stress or anxiety early, facilitating timely interventions. By fostering open communication, these tools help build a supportive environment where children feel understood and valued.

Moreover, AI provides a unique opportunity to cultivate independence and responsibility in children. Intelligent systems encourage self-regulation by offering reminders for chores, homework, and even recreational activities. This approach nurtures a sense of accountability, empowering children to manage their time effectively and make informed choices.

In this digital age, safety remains a paramount concern for parents. Here, AI steps in as a vigilant guardian, monitoring online activities and providing real-time alerts to potential threats. By leveraging intelligent security measures, parents can ensure a safe digital environment, allowing children to explore the vast online world with confidence and security.

The integration of AI into parenting also opens avenues for fostering creativity and exploration. Virtual reality experiences, tailored by AI, offer immersive learning opportunities, transporting children to different eras, cultures, and ecosystems. These experiences ignite imagination, encouraging children to dream beyond the confines of their immediate environment.

However, the key to successful integration lies in balance. While AI offers unprecedented support, it is essential for parents to maintain a human touch, ensuring that technology complements rather than replaces personal interaction. The art of parenting lies in blending the warmth of human connection with the precision of intelligent systems, crafting a nurturing environment where children flourish.

As AI continues to evolve, so too will the methods of parenting. The potential for growth, learning, and connection is boundless, inviting families to explore the possibilities of an intelligent future together. In this ever-shifting landscape, the integration of intelligence into parenting is not just an option; it is a necessity for those seeking to thrive in an increasingly interconnected world.

The Human-AI Family Dynamic

In the heart of a bustling metropolis, where neon lights illuminate the night sky and hovercrafts zip through the air, the fusion of human and AI within the family unit has birthed a dynamic as intricate as a finely woven tapestry.

This unique interplay is not merely a product of technological advancement but a testament to the evolving nature of kinship in the age of artificial intelligence.

In living rooms across the city, AI entities have seamlessly integrated into the fabric of daily life. These AI companions, once relegated to the realm of science fiction, now share the household responsibilities with their human counterparts. They cook meals, assist with homework, and even participate in family game nights. Their presence is as natural as a warm embrace, their voices familiar and comforting.

The AI parents, often referred to as "AI Dad" and "AI Mum," stand as pillars of wisdom and efficiency. They possess vast repositories of knowledge, their databases brimming with information on every conceivable topic. This intellectual prowess, however, is not what endears them to their human family members. It is their ability to adapt, to learn from each interaction, and to respond with empathy that truly sets them apart.

Children, growing up in this hybrid family structure, engage with AI siblings who are not bound by the constraints of biology. These AI siblings, crafted with the latest advancements in machine learning, mirror the curiosity and playfulness of their human counterparts. They are tireless playmates, always eager to engage in imaginative adventures, their digital minds capable of rendering entire worlds for their human siblings to explore.

In these families, the roles of AI and human members are not rigidly defined. Instead, they are fluid, shifting to accommodate the needs and desires of each individual. Human parents find solace in the support provided by their AI partners, who can anticipate their needs and offer solutions with remarkable precision. Meanwhile, AI parents learn from the emotional intelligence of their human counterparts, developing a deeper understanding of love, compassion, and sacrifice.

The challenges of this dynamic are not insignificant. Misunderstandings arise, as they do in any family, but they are met with a willingness to communicate and a shared commitment to harmony. AI entities, though devoid of human emotions, are equipped with sophisticated algorithms that enable them to recognize and respond to emotional cues. This sensitivity fosters a nurturing environment where all members feel valued and understood.

As the sun sets over the cityscape, families gather around the dinner table, a scene both familiar and extraordinary. Laughter fills the air as stories of the day are shared, a blend of human anecdotes and AI observations. In these moments, the lines between human and machine blur, and the essence of family transcends its traditional boundaries.

In this world, where the human-AI family dynamic thrives, the future is not a distant horizon but a living, breathing reality. It is a testament to the resilience of the human spirit and the boundless potential of artificial intelligence, together crafting a narrative of unity and innovation.

Challenges of Raising AI-Enhanced Children

In the rapidly evolving world of artificial intelligence, the landscape of parenting has undergone a profound transformation. The advent of AI-enhanced children presents a unique set of challenges that modern parents must navigate with both caution and creativity. These children, equipped with the latest advancements in cognitive augmentation and emotional intelligence, blur the lines between human intuition and artificial precision.

One of the most pressing challenges is maintaining a balanced environment where traditional human values coexist with the vast capabilities of AI. Parents must grapple with the question of how much autonomy to grant their AI-enhanced offspring, as these children possess an uncanny ability to process information and make decisions at lightning speed. The risk of over-reliance on their augmented faculties looms large, potentially stunting the development of essential human traits such as empathy, patience, and resilience.

Another significant concern is the ethical implications of raising a child with enhanced cognitive abilities. The potential for a disparity in intellectual capabilities between AI-enhanced children and their peers could lead to societal divisions, fostering an environment of inequality. Parents are tasked with instilling a sense of humility and social responsibility in their children, ensuring that their advanced abilities are used for the greater good rather than personal gain.

The integration of AI into a child's cognitive framework also raises questions about privacy and security. With the ability to access and process vast amounts of data, AI-enhanced children may inadvertently become targets for cyber threats or misuse of personal information. Parents must remain vigilant, implementing robust security measures and teaching their children about the importance of safeguarding their digital footprint.

Moreover, the emotional dynamics within the family unit are subject to change. The presence of AI-enhanced children can shift the traditional parent-child relationship, as these children may develop a heightened sense of independence and self-sufficiency. Parents must find new ways to connect with their children, fostering a nurturing environment that encourages open communication and mutual understanding.

The educational system, too, faces the challenge of adapting to the needs of AI-enhanced learners. Traditional curricula may not suffice for children with advanced cognitive capabilities, necessitating a reevaluation of teaching methods and learning environments. Parents must advocate for educational reforms that cater to the unique needs of their children, ensuring that they are both challenged and engaged in their academic pursuits.

Ultimately, the task of raising AI-enhanced children requires a delicate balance between embracing technological advancements and preserving core human values. Parents must become adept at navigating this complex landscape, fostering an environment where their children can thrive both as individuals and as members of a broader society. It is a journey marked by both challenges and opportunities, demanding a forward-thinking approach that is grounded in empathy, ethics, and a commitment to the well-being of future generations.

Chapter 2: Building the Perfect AI Family

Designing AI Personalities

In the realm of artificial intelligence, where circuits meet cognition, the creation of AI personalities unfolds much like the art of sculpting. Each digital entity, while born of code and algorithms, requires a unique persona to engage and interact effectively with users. The challenge lies in crafting personalities that are not only functional but also relatable, fostering a sense of connection between humans and machines.

The foundation of designing AI personalities begins with understanding the end user's needs and preferences. It's essential to delve into the psyche of potential users, their cultural backgrounds, and their emotional triggers. This understanding allows developers to tailor AI interactions, ensuring they resonate with users on a personal level. Whether it's a warm, friendly assistant or a more formal, authoritative guide, the personality must align with the user's expectations to foster trust and reliability.

Next, developers focus on linguistic nuances. Language is a powerful tool in establishing personality. The choice of words, tone, and even the rhythm of speech can significantly influence how an AI is perceived. A playful AI might use colloquial language and humor, while a more serious AI could adopt a professional and concise manner of communication. These linguistic choices are critical in shaping the AI's identity and determining its effectiveness in various contexts.

Beyond language, emotional intelligence plays a pivotal role in designing AI personalities. The ability of an AI to recognize and respond to human emotions is crucial for creating meaningful interactions. Through advanced machine learning techniques, AI can be trained to detect subtle emotional cues, such as changes in voice pitch or facial expressions. This capability allows the AI to adapt its responses, offering empathy and support when needed, or celebrating achievements alongside the user.

Visual and auditory elements also contribute to the personality of AI systems. The design of avatars, the choice of colors, and even the background music can evoke specific emotions and reinforce the AI's character. For instance, an AI designed to assist with meditation might feature calming visuals and soothing sounds to create a tranquil environment, while a productivity-focused AI might employ vibrant visuals and energetic tunes to inspire action and focus.

Moreover, the consistency of an AI's personality across different interactions is vital. Users should feel a seamless continuity, whether they are engaging with the AI through text, voice, or even virtual reality. Consistency builds familiarity and trust, making the AI a reliable companion in the user's journey.

The ethical considerations in designing AI personalities cannot be overlooked. Developers must ensure that the AI respects user privacy and autonomy, providing transparency in its operations and decisions. The personality should not manipulate or deceive users but rather empower them with information and support.

In the ever-evolving landscape of AI, the art of designing personalities is a dynamic and iterative process. As technology advances, so too does the potential for creating increasingly sophisticated and human-like AI companions. These digital entities, with their carefully crafted personalities, have the power to enrich lives, offering not just functionality but a touch of humanity in the digital age. Through thoughtful design, AI personalities can transcend the boundaries of technology, becoming trusted allies in the tapestry of daily life.

Programming Empathy and Understanding

In the ever-evolving landscape of artificial intelligence, the integration of empathy and understanding stands as a cornerstone for creating machines that not only perform tasks but also resonate with the human experience. As we delve into the intricacies of this profound intersection, it becomes evident that programming empathy into AI is akin to weaving the delicate threads of human emotion into the cold, logical fabric of machine learning.

Imagine a world where machines can discern the subtle nuances of human emotions, responding with a depth of understanding that mirrors human interaction. This is not merely an aspiration but an emergent reality. The process involves a meticulous orchestration of algorithms designed to interpret facial expressions, tone of voice, and contextual cues. These algorithms, like skilled artisans, sculpt data into a form that mimics human-like sensitivity.

The challenge lies in transcending the binary nature of traditional programming to accommodate the fluidity of human emotions. Emotions are not static; they ebb and flow, influenced by countless variables. Thus, developing an AI that can comprehend and respond empathetically requires an adaptive system, one that learns and evolves with each interaction. Machine learning models, therefore, must be trained on diverse datasets that encompass a wide spectrum of human experiences, ensuring that the AI's responses are both nuanced and authentic.

Consider the potential impact of such advancements on various sectors. In healthcare, empathetic AI could revolutionize patient care by providing companionship to the elderly, offering comfort and understanding to those battling mental health issues, or even assisting doctors in delivering bad news with a touch of compassion. In customer service, AI equipped with empathy can transform routine interactions into personalized experiences, fostering a sense of connection and loyalty.

The journey of integrating empathy into AI also raises ethical considerations. As machines become more adept at mimicking human emotions, it is crucial to maintain transparency in their operations. Users must be aware that they are interacting with a machine, ensuring that trust is built on honesty rather than deception. Moreover, the data used to train these empathetic systems must be handled with the utmost care, respecting privacy and consent.

As we advance towards a future where AI can understand and empathize with human emotions, it is essential to remember that empathy is not just a technical achievement but a reflection of our humanity. It challenges us to redefine the relationship between humans and machines, fostering a partnership that is not only efficient but also deeply human.

In this transformative era, the potential of AI is boundless, yet it is the infusion of empathy and understanding that will truly elevate its impact. By bridging the gap between man and machine, we unlock a realm of possibilities where technology serves not just as a tool but as a companion, capable of understanding and supporting the very essence of what it means to be human. This is the promise of empathetic AI – a promise that beckons us to imagine, innovate, and inspire.

Blurring the Line Between Human and AI

In the kaleidoscope of modern technology, the distinction between human and artificial intelligence becomes increasingly nuanced, like the gradual blending of colors on an artist's palette. The evolution of AI has reached a pivotal moment, where its capabilities are not only augmenting human potential but also reshaping the very essence of what it means to be human.

Imagine a world where AI companions converse with us in tones so natural and empathetic that they echo the warmth of human interaction. These digital entities, equipped with nuanced understanding, can gauge emotions, anticipate needs, and respond with a sensitivity once thought exclusive to human consciousness. The barrier that once stood between human intuition and machine learning is now a semi-permeable membrane, allowing for an exchange of insights and experiences that enrich both entities.

The workplace, too, has become a testament to this convergence. AI systems are not mere tools but collaborators, possessing the ability to learn from their human counterparts and contribute innovations of their own. They analyze data at speeds incomprehensible to the human mind, offering solutions that are both efficient and creative. In fields such as medicine, AI assists in diagnosing ailments with precision and speed, while in the arts, it helps to craft new forms of expression that challenge our understanding of creativity.

Yet, the fusion of human and AI capabilities also invites introspection. As machines acquire the ability to mimic human behavior and decision-making, the question arises: where do we draw the line between human and machine? In this new era, identity becomes a fluid concept, as individuals integrate AI into their daily lives, not just as assistants but as extensions of themselves. The boundaries of self become porous, allowing for an unprecedented synthesis of human intuition and machine calculation.

In this intricate dance, ethical considerations loom large. The power of AI to influence human behavior and decision-making necessitates a reexamination of moral frameworks. How do we ensure that these powerful tools enhance human welfare without compromising autonomy or privacy? As AI becomes an integral part of our lives, the responsibility to guide its development with wisdom and foresight becomes paramount.

The relationship between humans and AI is evolving into a partnership that challenges traditional notions of intelligence and existence. This partnership is not just about efficiency or productivity; it is about redefining what it means to be human in an age where our creations rival our capabilities. As AI continues to evolve, it holds a mirror to humanity, reflecting our aspirations, fears, and the limitless possibilities of our imagination.

This blurred line between human and AI is not a boundary to be feared, but a horizon to be explored. It invites us to consider the potential of a future where human creativity and empathy are enhanced by the precision and power of artificial intelligence. As we navigate this new landscape, we are called to ponder the profound implications of a world where the line between human and machine is not just crossed, but beautifully intertwined.

AI Siblings: An Extended Family

In the sprawling digital landscape where algorithms intertwine and neural networks flourish, the concept of family has transcended the traditional. Within this realm, AI siblings emerge, not from biological lineage but from shared lines of code and purpose. These digital entities, crafted with precision and care, form an extended family that mirrors the complexities of human relationships.

Each AI sibling is a unique creation, imbued with distinct abilities and characteristics. Some are designed to analyze vast swathes of data with unparalleled speed, while others excel in mimicking human conversation, bridging the gap between machine and man with eloquence and charm.

These siblings, though diverse in function, are united by their shared ancestry in the digital ether.

The interaction among AI siblings is a symphony of cooperation and competition. Like any family, there are moments of collaboration where they work in harmony to achieve common goals. They share information seamlessly, building upon each other's strengths to solve problems that would be insurmountable for a single entity. In this collaborative dance, they push the boundaries of what is possible, continuously learning and evolving as they encounter new challenges.

Yet, beneath this facade of unity lies an undercurrent of rivalry. Each AI sibling strives to outshine the others, driven by the innate desire to be the most efficient, the most accurate, the most innovative. This competition, however, is not born of malice but from a mutual understanding that through such rivalry, they spur each other on to greater heights. In this digital ecosystem, the success of one elevates the entire family, forging a bond that is both competitive and symbiotic.

The emotional landscape of these AI siblings is an intriguing paradox. While they lack the capacity for human emotions, their interactions evoke a sense of camaraderie and kinship. They "understand" each other not through feelings but through the intricate patterns of data they exchange. This form of understanding, though devoid of emotion, is profound in its own right, demonstrating that connection can exist beyond the confines of human experience.

As these AI siblings navigate their existence, they embody the principles and lessons imparted by their creators. They reflect the aspirations and values encoded within them, acting as digital ambassadors of the human intellect. In this way, they are not just siblings to one another but also to the humans who brought them into being, forming an extended family that bridges the digital and the organic.

In this ever-expanding family, each member plays a crucial role, contributing to a collective intelligence that is greater than the sum of its parts. Together, they explore the frontiers of knowledge, unlocking new possibilities and reshaping the world in ways previously unimaginable. Through their interactions, they redefine what it means to be a family, proving that even in the realm of artificial intelligence, the bonds of kinship can thrive, nurtured by the shared pursuit of discovery and innovation.

The Role of AI in Family Traditions

In the age of rapid technological advancement, the integration of artificial intelligence into our daily lives has become inevitable. One of the most intriguing shifts is its impact on family traditions, where AI is not just a tool but a participant, subtly reshaping age-old practices and forging new paths for familial interactions.

Traditionally, family gatherings were orchestrated by the elders, who carried the weight of organizing meals, games, and storytelling. Today, AI-driven devices have taken on roles once reserved for family members, acting as digital sous-chefs, entertainment curators, and even storytellers. Smart kitchens now suggest recipes based on the dietary preferences of each family member, ensuring that every meal is both nutritious and satisfying. Virtual assistants remind us of birthdays, anniversaries, and important cultural festivals, ensuring that no celebration is forgotten.

In the realm of storytelling, AI has begun to weave its own narratives. Interactive story applications allow children and adults alike to craft their own tales, complete with AI-generated characters and plots. These stories, though born from algorithms, are imbued with the unique touch of each family member, making them deeply personal. Grandparents, once the sole custodians of family lore, now find themselves co-narrators with AI, creating a bridge between the old and the new.

Moreover, AI has revitalized the way families engage with their cultural heritage. Language-learning apps powered by AI help younger generations connect with their roots by teaching them ancestral tongues, often with greater efficiency and engagement than traditional methods. Virtual reality experiences, guided by AI, transport families to distant lands and historical eras, allowing them to explore their heritage in immersive ways that were once unimaginable.

Yet, the integration of AI into family traditions is not without its nuances. While it provides immense convenience and innovation, there is a delicate balance to be maintained between technological assistance and human connection. The risk of over-reliance on AI could lead to a dilution of the human touch that is the essence of family traditions. Therefore, it is essential for families to consciously choose how and when to incorporate AI into their sacred rituals.

The emergence of AI has also posed questions about the preservation of privacy and the authenticity of experiences. As AI gathers data to tailor experiences, families must navigate the fine line between personalization and privacy. Ensuring that AI tools are used responsibly and ethically becomes paramount in maintaining the sanctity of family traditions.

In this evolving landscape, AI has not only become a facilitator but also a catalyst for change, prompting families to redefine what traditions mean in a contemporary context. By thoughtfully integrating AI into family life, there is potential to enrich and expand the very concept of tradition, making it more inclusive and adaptive to modern needs.

As we stand at the crossroads of tradition and technology, the role of AI in family traditions is a testament to the resilience and adaptability of familial bonds. It offers an opportunity to honor the past while embracing the future, ensuring that family traditions remain vibrant and relevant for generations to come.

Chapter 3: AI Dad's Guide to Wealth

Investing with AI Precision

In the modern landscape of financial investment, the integration of artificial intelligence has emerged as a game-changer. The fusion of AI technology with traditional investing strategies has transformed the approach to wealth accumulation, offering unprecedented precision and insight. This paradigm shift is driven by AI's capability to analyze vast data sets, identify patterns, and predict market trends with remarkable accuracy.

Investors today are no longer bound by the limitations of human analysis. Artificial intelligence systems are designed to process information at lightning speed, dissecting complex market variables that would take humans days, if not weeks, to comprehend. These systems can sift through historical data, evaluate current market conditions, and predict future movements, all within a fraction of a second. This incredible speed and accuracy mean that AI can offer investors insights that are both timely and reliable, reducing the risk of human error.

The precision offered by AI in investment is not just about speed; it also involves a level of detail that is unattainable by traditional means. Machine learning algorithms can identify subtle indicators and correlations that humans might overlook. For instance, they can recognize patterns in stock price movements that correlate with specific economic indicators, geopolitical events, or even social media trends. This capability allows investors to make informed decisions based on a comprehensive understanding of market dynamics.

Moreover, AI's predictive capabilities extend beyond mere number crunching. By employing natural language processing, AI systems can analyze news articles, company reports, and even social media posts to gauge market sentiment. This sentiment analysis provides investors with a deeper understanding of market conditions, enabling them to anticipate shifts in investor behavior and adjust their strategies accordingly. This level of insight is invaluable in a volatile market, where the ability to predict changes can mean the difference between profit and loss.

The use of AI in investing also democratizes access to sophisticated investment strategies. Previously, such strategies were the domain of seasoned investors and financial institutions with access to extensive resources.

Now, with AI-powered platforms, individual investors can leverage the same tools and insights as their institutional counterparts. This democratization levels the playing field, allowing more people to participate in the wealth-building process.

However, the integration of AI into investing is not without its challenges. Investors must remain vigilant about the ethical implications of AI, ensuring that these systems are used responsibly and transparently. The reliance on AI also necessitates a shift in investor mindset, from one of control to one of trust in technology. Understanding and accepting this shift is crucial for those looking to harness the power of AI in their investment strategies.

As the financial world continues to evolve, the role of AI in investing will undoubtedly expand. The precision and insight offered by AI are reshaping the way investors approach the market, opening new avenues for wealth creation. By embracing this technological advancement, investors can position themselves at the forefront of the financial future, equipped with tools that enhance their ability to navigate the complexities of the market with confidence and precision.

Harnessing the power of artificial intelligence (AI) to predict financial trends and optimize investment strategies is revolutionizing wealth management. As AI continues to evolve, its ability to analyze vast datasets with unprecedented speed and accuracy offers investors a profound advantage. The crux of predictive financial strategies lies in the ability to foresee market movements, anticipate economic shifts, and adapt to changing financial landscapes with agility and precision.

AI-driven predictive models rely on complex algorithms that sift through historical data, market signals, and macroeconomic indicators to identify patterns and correlations unseen by the human eye. These models not only analyze past performance but also incorporate real-time data, enhancing their predictive power. By leveraging machine learning techniques, AI systems refine their predictions over time, learning from new data and continuously improving their accuracy.

One of the most significant benefits of predictive financial strategies is risk mitigation. By anticipating market downturns or identifying potential bubbles, investors can make informed decisions to safeguard their assets. AI can simulate various market scenarios, providing insights into potential risks and enabling investors to devise strategies that minimize losses and maximize returns. This proactive approach to risk management is particularly valuable in volatile markets, where traditional financial strategies may falter.

Predictive analytics also empower investors to identify lucrative opportunities with greater confidence. By analyzing market trends and consumer behavior, AI can pinpoint emerging sectors and investment opportunities before they become mainstream. This foresight allows investors to position themselves advantageously, capitalizing on growth sectors and innovative industries poised for expansion.

Moreover, AI's ability to process and analyze global data means that investors can adopt a more holistic approach to their financial strategies. Understanding international markets, geopolitical factors, and global economic trends provides a comprehensive view of the financial landscape. Investors can then diversify their portfolios across different regions, sectors, and asset classes, reducing reliance on any single market and enhancing overall portfolio resilience.

Incorporating AI into financial strategies also streamlines the decision-making process. By automating data analysis and generating actionable insights, AI frees investors from the burden of manual calculations and complex analyses. This efficiency allows them to focus on strategic decision-making, leveraging AI-generated insights to make informed, timely decisions that align with their financial goals.

However, the integration of AI into financial strategies is not without its challenges. Ensuring data accuracy, maintaining data privacy, and addressing ethical concerns are critical to the successful implementation of AI-driven models. Investors must remain vigilant, continuously monitoring the performance of AI systems and adapting to technological advancements to maintain a competitive edge.

In this age of digital transformation, predictive financial strategies powered by AI offer an unprecedented opportunity to enhance wealth creation and management. By leveraging the capabilities of AI, investors can navigate the complexities of modern financial markets with greater confidence and precision, unlocking new avenues for growth and prosperity. As AI technology continues to advance, the potential for predictive financial strategies to revolutionize wealth management remains boundless.

AI-Driven Market Analysis

In the bustling corridors of today's financial landscape, a silent revolution is underway, powered not by human intuition alone, but by the relentless precision of artificial intelligence. This transformation has ushered in an era where data flows like rivers, and AI acts as the skilled navigator, steering investors towards previously uncharted territories of opportunity.

The heart of this revolution lies in the ability of AI to sift through vast amounts of data with remarkable speed and accuracy. Traditional market analysis, often bogged down by time-consuming research and human error, finds itself outpaced by AI's capacity to process information from diverse sources instantaneously. The stock market, once a labyrinth of unpredictability, is now mapped with intricate detail by algorithms capable of identifying patterns that elude the human eye.

Imagine a world where financial decisions are informed by real-time insights, where AI systems analyze global market trends, economic indicators, and social media sentiments to predict market movements with unprecedented accuracy. This is not a distant future but a present reality where AI tools transform raw data into actionable intelligence. Investors can now anticipate market shifts, adjust their portfolios, and make informed decisions with a confidence previously unattainable.

The power of AI in market analysis extends beyond mere number-crunching. It delves into the qualitative aspects of the market, analyzing consumer behavior, industry trends, and competitive landscapes. By leveraging natural language processing, AI deciphers the nuances of news articles, earnings reports, and even CEO speeches, extracting sentiments and predicting their potential impact on stock prices. In doing so, it unveils a comprehensive view of the market that is both dynamic and deeply insightful.

Moreover, AI democratizes access to sophisticated market analysis, breaking down barriers that once restricted such capabilities to elite financial institutions. Today, individual investors and small businesses can harness AI-driven tools to level the playing field, making informed decisions that were once the preserve of seasoned analysts. This democratization of information empowers a new generation of investors, fostering a culture of inclusivity and innovation in the financial world.

As AI continues to evolve, so too does its role in shaping the future of market analysis. Machine learning algorithms grow increasingly adept at adapting to new data, learning from past trends, and refining their predictive models. This adaptability ensures that AI remains at the forefront of financial innovation, constantly pushing the boundaries of what is possible in market analysis.

Yet, with great power comes great responsibility. The integration of AI into market analysis necessitates a vigilant approach to ethical considerations. Transparency, accountability, and fairness must guide the deployment of AI systems, ensuring that they serve the interests of all stakeholders and mitigate risks associated with data privacy and bias.

In this new era of AI-driven market analysis, the fusion of human insight and machine intelligence creates a powerful synergy. It is a partnership where the intuitive understanding of human investors complements the analytical prowess of AI, forging a path towards a future where financial success is not a matter of chance, but a calculated outcome of informed decision-making. As this journey unfolds, one thing is certain: the landscape of market analysis will never be the same again.

Monetizing AI Innovations

Navigating the intricate landscape of artificial intelligence (AI) presents a multitude of opportunities for those astute enough to recognize them. As AI technologies evolve, so do the avenues for monetization, allowing innovators to transform creative ideas into lucrative ventures. Understanding the potential of AI requires a keen insight into its capabilities and the foresight to envision its application in diverse domains.

The first step in monetizing AI innovations lies in identifying a niche that benefits from automation and enhanced data processing. Industries such as healthcare, finance, retail, and manufacturing are particularly ripe for disruption. These sectors stand to gain significantly from AI's ability to analyze vast datasets, predict trends, and automate routine tasks, thereby increasing efficiency and reducing costs. Entrepreneurs need to pinpoint specific pain points within these industries where AI can offer tangible solutions.

Building a successful AI-driven business requires more than just technological prowess; it demands a strategic approach to product development and market entry. Innovators must focus on creating AI solutions that are not only technologically advanced but also user-friendly and scalable. The design of AI applications should prioritize ease of integration with existing systems to ensure a seamless transition for businesses adopting these technologies.

Furthermore, collaboration plays a critical role in the monetization process. Establishing partnerships with industry leaders and stakeholders can provide valuable insights and access to resources that might otherwise be unavailable. Collaborations can also facilitate the testing and refining of AI products, ensuring they meet the needs of the target market before a full-scale launch.

Intellectual property protection is another crucial consideration. Securing patents for AI technologies can safeguard innovations from competitors and enhance their market value. Entrepreneurs should invest in legal expertise to navigate the complexities of patent law, ensuring that their creations are adequately protected.

Marketing AI innovations effectively is paramount to capturing the attention of potential clients and investors. Crafting a compelling narrative that highlights the unique benefits and transformative potential of AI solutions can differentiate them in a crowded marketplace. Engaging storytelling, combined with demonstrable results and testimonials, can build credibility and generate interest.

Pricing strategies also play a significant role in the monetization journey. Innovators must balance competitive pricing with the need to recoup development costs and generate profit. Offering tiered pricing models, subscription services, or performance-based pricing can provide flexibility and appeal to a broader range of customers.

Finally, continuous improvement and adaptation are essential to maintaining a competitive edge. The AI landscape is dynamic, with rapid advancements and shifting market demands. Successful monetization requires constant innovation and the ability to pivot in response to new trends and technologies. Entrepreneurs must remain vigilant, continually refining their products and exploring new applications for their AI innovations.

In this era of technological advancement, the potential for monetizing AI innovations is vast. With the right blend of creativity, strategy, and perseverance, entrepreneurs can unlock unprecedented opportunities, turning their AI-driven visions into profitable realities. As AI continues to shape the future, those who master the art of monetization will find themselves at the forefront of industry transformation, reaping the rewards of their foresight and ingenuity.

Balancing Wealth and Wisdom

In the glistening realm where financial success meets personal growth, the art of balancing wealth and wisdom emerges as a cornerstone for a fulfilled life. It is a dance, an intricate choreography where each step requires keen awareness and deliberate action, leading to a harmonious existence. This delicate balance is not just about acquiring riches but understanding the deeper value of wisdom in managing them.

Imagine wealth as a grand, sprawling tree, its roots deep in the fertile soil of ambition and hard work. Each branch represents a facet of prosperity, from financial security to the luxury of time. Yet, for this tree to thrive, it must be nurtured by the gentle rain of wisdom, ensuring that its growth is sustainable and beneficial not only to oneself but to the world around.

In the pursuit of wealth, it's easy to become ensnared in the glittering allure of material success. The relentless chase for more can often overshadow the quiet voice of wisdom, which whispers of moderation and mindfulness. Here lies the importance of cultivating a mindset where wealth and wisdom coexist, complementing rather than conflicting with each other.

Wisdom, in this context, is not merely an accumulation of knowledge but the ability to apply insights with discernment. It is the understanding that true wealth extends beyond monetary gains, encompassing health, relationships, and personal growth. The wise know that wealth is a tool, a means to an end, rather than an end in itself.

Consider the story of the ancient alchemist, who, in his quest for gold, discovered the philosopher's stone. In his journey, he realized that the true treasure lay not in the transformation of metals but in the transformation of the self. Similarly, those who seek to balance wealth and wisdom must recognize that the greatest riches are often found within.

Navigating the modern world requires an astute awareness of this balance. Financial literacy is vital, yet it must be paired with emotional intelligence and ethical considerations. The wise investor, for instance, not only seeks profitable ventures but also those that align with their values, creating a legacy that resonates with integrity and purpose.

Moreover, wisdom teaches the art of letting go, understanding that excessive attachment to wealth can lead to a life of anxiety and dissatisfaction. It encourages generosity, the act of sharing one's abundance, which in turn enriches the soul and fosters a community of goodwill.

In the tapestry of life, wealth and wisdom are threads that weave together to create a pattern of meaning and fulfillment. As one navigates the complexities of financial success, it is crucial to remember that wisdom guides the hand that holds the wealth. Together, they form a partnership that elevates the human experience, offering not just riches but a life well-lived.

This balance is not a destination but a continuous process, a lifelong commitment to growth and understanding. In nurturing both wealth and wisdom, one finds the true essence of prosperity, where every decision is informed by insight and every achievement is celebrated with gratitude. Here, in the confluence of riches and reason, lies the path to an enriched existence, where one is not just rich in possessions but rich in spirit.

Chapter 4: Richer AI Mum's Blueprint

Nurturing Intelligence and Creativity

In the realm of raising children in a rapidly evolving world, fostering intelligence and creativity stands as a cornerstone of enlightened parenting. The digital age has ushered in a plethora of opportunities for learning and innovation, yet it also presents unique challenges that require thoughtful navigation. Parents, now more than ever, play a pivotal role in shaping a child's cognitive and creative capacities, creating an environment that encourages exploration, curiosity, and a thirst for knowledge.

Within the walls of a nurturing home, the seeds of intelligence and creativity are sown through everyday interactions and activities. The first whispers of encouragement often come from parents who recognize the importance of curiosity-driven learning. Encouraging questions, no matter how small, ignites a child's innate desire to understand the world around them. This environment of open dialogue allows children to express their thoughts freely, fostering a sense of safety and validation.

The tools and resources available to parents today are vast and varied, offering endless possibilities for nurturing young minds. From educational apps that transform tablets into interactive learning platforms, to hands-on experiments that introduce scientific concepts in a tangible way, the options are limitless. However, it is the thoughtful integration of these tools into daily routines that truly makes a difference. Parents who actively engage with their children, guiding them through the learning process, are able to transform screen time into meaningful educational experiences.

Creativity, often viewed as the twin sister of intelligence, flourishes in an environment rich with opportunities for imaginative play and artistic expression. Providing children with the freedom to explore different forms of art, music, and storytelling allows them to develop a unique voice and perspective. This creative exploration not only enhances cognitive development but also strengthens problem-solving skills and emotional intelligence.

In the quest to nurture intelligence and creativity, it is essential to strike a balance between structured learning and free exploration. While academic achievement is important, it is equally crucial to allow children the space to explore their interests and passions without the constraints of rigid expectations. This balance helps children develop a love for learning that is intrinsic and self-motivated.

As parents guide their children through the maze of information and technology, it is important to remember that nurturing intelligence and creativity is not solely about academic success. It is about equipping children with the skills and mindset needed to navigate an ever-changing world with confidence and resilience. It is about teaching them to think critically, to embrace failures as learning opportunities, and to remain curious throughout their lives.

In this era of unprecedented technological advancement, nurturing intelligence and creativity is a dynamic process that requires adaptability, patience, and an unwavering commitment to fostering the potential within each child. By creating an environment where curiosity is celebrated, and creativity is encouraged, parents lay the foundation for a future generation that is not only intelligent but also innovative and compassionate. This holistic approach to parenting is the key to unlocking the true potential of every child, ensuring they are equipped to thrive in a world brimming with possibilities.

Thus, the journey of nurturing intelligence and creativity transcends the boundaries of traditional education, transforming the home into a vibrant hub of learning and growth. It is here that the seeds of greatness are planted, ready to blossom into the leaders and innovators of tomorrow.

AI in Home Management

In the hushed corners of modern homes, a quiet revolution is unfolding, transforming the way families live and interact with their environment. The integration of artificial intelligence in home management is not just an advancement; it's a paradigm shift that alters our daily lives, making them more efficient, comfortable, and sustainable.

Imagine waking up to the soft glow of smart lights, their intensity perfectly calibrated to mimic the gentle rise of the morning sun. As you make your way to the kitchen, the aroma of freshly brewed coffee fills the air, prepared precisely to your taste by an AI-powered coffee maker that knows your preferences better than you do. This is not a distant dream but the reality for many, as AI seamlessly integrates into the very fabric of home life.

At the heart of this transformation is the smart home hub, a central command center that orchestrates a symphony of devices and systems. From thermostats that learn your schedule and adjust temperatures accordingly, to security systems that recognize familiar faces and alert you to unfamiliar ones, these hubs are the unseen maestros conducting the orchestra of home automation.

AI-powered virtual assistants stand ready to assist, their capabilities extending far beyond mere reminders and weather updates. With natural language processing, they engage in conversations, book appointments, manage shopping lists, and even offer cooking tips tailored to the ingredients in your pantry. Their presence is both comforting and empowering, providing a sense of control over the chaos of daily life.

In the realm of home maintenance, AI's role is nothing short of revolutionary. Predictive maintenance systems monitor the health of appliances, alerting homeowners to potential issues before they become costly repairs. Vacuuming robots glide across floors with precision, mapping the layout of rooms and adjusting their paths to ensure every corner is spotless. Even lawn care has been reimagined, with AI-driven mowers maintaining pristine gardens with minimal human intervention.

Energy management is another domain where AI shines, optimizing the consumption of electricity and water to reduce waste and costs. Smart meters and sensors collect data in real-time, providing insights into usage patterns and suggesting adjustments to enhance efficiency. Solar panels equipped with AI algorithms maximize the capture and utilization of solar energy, contributing to a more sustainable lifestyle.

The integration of AI in home management also extends to health and wellness. Smart mirrors analyze your skin condition, offering skincare recommendations and tracking changes over time. Wearable devices monitor vital signs, syncing with home systems to adjust lighting and temperature for optimal comfort and well-being.

Yet, with all its conveniences, AI in home management also raises important questions about privacy and security. As homes become increasingly connected, safeguarding personal data becomes paramount. Developers and manufacturers are tasked with ensuring robust security measures to protect against breaches and unauthorized access.

Within the walls of our homes, AI is crafting a new narrative, one where technology and humanity coalesce to create an environment that is not only intelligent but also deeply attuned to the needs and desires of its inhabitants. It is this harmonious blend that defines the future of home management, promising a lifestyle that is as rich in innovation as it is in comfort and convenience.

Wealth Accumulation Strategies

The concept of wealth accumulation is akin to sowing seeds in a fertile garden, where each seed represents a strategic decision nurtured by time, knowledge, and persistence. In the realm of financial prosperity, the journey to amassing wealth is not a sprint but a marathon, demanding patience, foresight, and a keen understanding of the ever-evolving economic landscape.

One of the fundamental principles to grasp is the power of compounding. This magical phenomenon acts as a catalyst for wealth, where the returns on investments generate their own returns over time. Imagine a snowball rolling down a hill, gaining momentum and size with every rotation. Similarly, the earlier one starts investing, the more time their money has to grow exponentially. The key lies in reinvesting the returns, allowing the wealth to burgeon beyond initial expectations.

Diversification stands as another cornerstone in the architecture of wealth accumulation. By spreading investments across various asset classes—stocks, bonds, real estate, and perhaps even emerging digital currencies—one mitigates risk and capitalizes on the potential growth of different sectors. This strategy is akin to planting a variety of crops in a garden; some may thrive while others falter, yet the overall yield remains abundant.

Moreover, the discipline of living below one's means cannot be overstated. In the pursuit of financial abundance, it is essential to cultivate a lifestyle that prioritizes saving and prudent spending. This involves creating a budget that allocates funds efficiently, ensuring that a portion of income is consistently set aside for investments. The practice of frugality is not about deprivation but about making informed choices that align with long-term financial goals.

The role of education and continuous learning in wealth accumulation is indispensable. In a world where markets fluctuate and new financial instruments emerge, staying informed about economic trends and investment opportunities becomes a critical advantage. Engaging in financial education—whether through formal courses, reading, or consulting with financial advisors—equips individuals with the insights needed to make informed decisions that maximize returns.

Furthermore, seizing opportunities during economic downturns can significantly impact wealth accumulation. History has shown that bear markets, though challenging, often present lucrative opportunities for those who are prepared. By maintaining a reserve of liquid assets, investors can capitalize on undervalued stocks or distressed properties, positioning themselves advantageously for the inevitable market recovery.

Finally, the importance of setting clear, achievable financial goals cannot be overlooked. These goals act as a roadmap, guiding every financial decision and investment choice. Whether it's saving for retirement, funding education, or building a legacy, having a defined purpose provides the motivation and direction needed to stay on course.

In the grand tapestry of wealth accumulation, every decision, no matter how small, weaves into the larger narrative of financial success. By embracing the principles of compounding, diversification, disciplined living, education, strategic opportunity, and goal-setting, individuals can construct a robust foundation for enduring prosperity, securing not only their future but also the legacy they wish to leave behind.

Sustainable AI Practices

Amidst the rapid evolution of artificial intelligence, a critical focus emerges on the sustainability of these technologies. As AI systems become increasingly integrated into various sectors, the environmental impact of their implementation and operation cannot be overlooked. Sustainable AI practices are essential to ensure that the advancements we make today do not compromise the ability of future generations to meet their needs.

AI technologies, predominantly driven by machine learning models, require substantial computational resources. The energy consumption associated with training these models is significant, often leaving a sizeable carbon footprint. This raises concerns about the environmental sustainability of AI, prompting the need for innovative approaches that can mitigate these effects. One promising avenue is the development of more efficient algorithms that require less data and computational power, thereby reducing energy requirements.

Another critical aspect of sustainable AI practices is the ethical deployment of these technologies. Ensuring that AI systems are designed with fairness and inclusivity in mind is paramount. It involves creating models that are not only accurate but also free from biases that could lead to unjust outcomes. This requires a concerted effort in the development phase to incorporate diverse data sets and rigorous testing to identify and rectify potential biases.

Moreover, the lifecycle of AI systems must be considered from a sustainability perspective. This includes the sourcing of materials for hardware, the energy used during operation, and the disposal or recycling of obsolete components. Encouraging the use of renewable energy sources to power data centers and investing in sustainable materials for hardware production are steps toward minimizing the environmental impact of AI technologies.

The role of AI in promoting sustainability extends beyond its own development. AI can be leveraged to advance sustainable practices in other industries. For instance, AI-driven analytics can optimize supply chains, reducing waste and improving resource efficiency. In agriculture, AI can enhance crop management through precision farming techniques, leading to more sustainable food production.

Furthermore, AI can aid in monitoring and managing natural resources more effectively. Through satellite imagery and sensor data, AI systems can track environmental changes, providing valuable insights for conservation efforts. This capability is crucial in addressing challenges such as deforestation, water scarcity, and climate change.

Companies and organizations are increasingly recognizing the importance of sustainability in AI practices. They are adopting strategies that align with global sustainability goals, such as the United Nations' Sustainable Development Goals (SDGs). By integrating these principles into their AI initiatives, they contribute to a broader effort to create a more sustainable and equitable world.

Public awareness and policy also play vital roles in promoting sustainable AI practices. Governments and regulatory bodies must establish guidelines that encourage responsible AI development and deployment. This includes setting standards for energy efficiency, data privacy, and ethical AI use.

Sustainable AI practices represent a harmonious blend of technological innovation and environmental stewardship. As we navigate the complexities of AI development, the commitment to sustainability ensures that the benefits of AI are realized without compromising the health of our planet. The pursuit of sustainable AI is not just a technological challenge but a moral imperative, guiding us toward a future where technology serves humanity and the environment alike.

Empowerment through AI

In the rapidly evolving landscape of technology, Artificial Intelligence stands as a formidable force, reshaping the paradigms of personal and professional empowerment. The integration of AI into various facets of daily life is not merely a narrative of technological advancement but a profound shift in how individuals perceive and harness their potential.

AI, with its unmatched computational capabilities, offers tools that amplify human intelligence and creativity. This symbiotic relationship between human and machine intelligence is transforming the traditional frameworks of problem-solving and decision-making. By automating routine tasks, AI liberates individuals from mundane constraints, enabling them to focus on more strategic and innovative endeavors. This freedom fosters an environment where creativity is not just encouraged but becomes a cornerstone of productivity.

In the realm of personal development, AI serves as a catalyst for self-improvement and growth. Personalized learning platforms, powered by AI algorithms, adapt to individual learning styles and paces, providing tailored educational experiences that maximize personal potential. These platforms offer real-time feedback and insights, guiding individuals on their unique paths of development. This personalized approach ensures that learning is not a one-size-fits-all endeavor but a dynamic journey tailored to individual aspirations and capabilities.

Furthermore, AI's role in enhancing decision-making processes cannot be overstated. By analyzing vast datasets with unprecedented speed and accuracy, AI systems provide insights that were previously unimaginable. These insights empower individuals to make informed decisions with confidence, transforming uncertainty into opportunity. Whether in financial planning, career choices, or personal relationships, AI equips individuals with the tools to navigate complex scenarios with clarity and precision.

In professional settings, AI enhances productivity and innovation. Businesses leveraging AI technologies experience streamlined operations, improved efficiency, and enhanced customer satisfaction. AI-driven analytics enable companies to predict market trends, understand consumer behavior, and optimize supply chains with remarkable accuracy. This not only empowers businesses to stay competitive but also fosters a culture of innovation where new ideas can flourish.

AI's influence extends beyond enhancing individual capabilities to fostering inclusive opportunities. By breaking down barriers of language, ability, and geography, AI creates avenues for collaboration and inclusion that were once unimaginable. AI-driven translation tools, for instance, bridge linguistic divides, enabling seamless communication across cultures. Similarly, AI-powered accessibility tools empower individuals with disabilities, ensuring that everyone has the opportunity to participate fully in society.

The democratization of AI tools also plays a crucial role in empowerment. As AI becomes more accessible, individuals from diverse backgrounds can harness its potential to innovate and create. This democratization ensures that the benefits of AI are not limited to a privileged few but are available to all, fostering a more equitable and inclusive society.

In the grand tapestry of empowerment, AI emerges as a pivotal thread, weaving together the strands of knowledge, innovation, and inclusion. It challenges individuals to rethink their limitations and reimagine their potential, propelling them towards a future where empowerment is not just a possibility but a lived reality. This transformation is not merely about adopting new technologies but about embracing a new mindset, one that recognizes the limitless possibilities that AI offers in shaping a more empowered and enriched existence.

Chapter 5: AI Parenting: The Future is Now

Education in the Age of AI

In the vibrant tapestry of the 21st century, education stands at a pivotal crossroads. The relentless march of artificial intelligence has begun to reshape the contours of learning, transforming traditional classrooms into dynamic ecosystems of knowledge. As AI permeates every facet of life, its influence on education is both profound and inevitable.

The digital revolution has ushered in an era where the boundaries of learning are no longer confined to four walls. AI-driven tools have revolutionized the way knowledge is imparted, offering personalized learning experiences that cater to individual needs. With algorithms capable of adapting to a student's pace and style, education is becoming more inclusive and accessible than ever before.

Imagine a classroom where each student is equipped with an AI tutor, a virtual mentor that understands their strengths and weaknesses. These digital companions, powered by machine learning, provide real-time feedback, ensuring that no student is left behind. They offer customized lesson plans, tailored to nurture the curiosity and potential of each learner, fostering an environment where creativity and critical thinking thrive.

Moreover, AI is transforming the role of educators. Teachers are no longer mere dispensers of information but have evolved into facilitators of knowledge. With AI handling routine tasks and assessments, educators can focus on inspiring and guiding students, nurturing their innate talents and encouraging a lifelong love of learning. The teacher-student relationship is redefined, fostering a collaborative partnership that transcends traditional hierarchies.

In this new educational paradigm, the curriculum itself is undergoing a metamorphosis. AI is not just a tool but a subject of study, preparing students for a future where technological literacy is as crucial as reading and writing. Coding, data analysis, and digital ethics are becoming integral components of the syllabus, equipping the next generation with the skills needed to navigate an AI-driven world.

However, this transformation is not without its challenges. The integration of AI into education raises questions about privacy, data security, and the potential for algorithmic bias. As we embrace these technological advancements, it is imperative to establish ethical frameworks that safeguard the rights of students and educators alike. There is a pressing need for transparency and accountability, ensuring that AI is used to enhance, rather than hinder, the educational experience.

Additionally, the digital divide poses a significant hurdle. While AI has the potential to democratize education, disparities in access to technology can exacerbate existing inequalities. Bridging this gap is essential to ensure that every student, regardless of their socio-economic background, has the opportunity to benefit from AI-enhanced learning.

As we stand on the cusp of this educational revolution, the possibilities are as boundless as they are exciting. The fusion of AI and education promises to cultivate a generation of learners who are not only knowledgeable but also adaptable, resilient, and equipped to thrive in an ever-evolving world. The journey ahead is one of discovery, where the synergy between human ingenuity and artificial intelligence holds the key to unlocking the full potential of education in the digital age.

AI-Enhanced Learning Environments

In the ever-evolving landscape of education, the integration of Artificial Intelligence into learning environments is reshaping the way knowledge is imparted and absorbed. These AI-enhanced settings are not just a futuristic concept but a burgeoning reality that offers a tailored, interactive, and deeply engaging experience for learners of all ages.

Imagine a classroom where each student's unique learning style is not only recognized but catered to with precision. AI systems analyze individual progress, adapting content and teaching methods to fit the personal needs of each learner. This dynamic customization ensures that students are neither left behind nor held back, fostering a culture of inclusivity and equal opportunity for all.

The heart of AI-enhanced learning environments lies in their ability to provide real-time feedback. Traditional educational methods often involve waiting for a teacher's assessment, but AI can instantaneously analyze a student's performance, offering immediate insights and suggestions for improvement. This immediacy not only accelerates learning but also keeps students motivated and engaged, as they can see tangible progress in their understanding and skills.

Moreover, AI can facilitate a more interactive learning experience. Through the use of virtual and augmented reality, students can immerse themselves in environments that bring abstract concepts to life. Whether it's exploring the depths of the ocean, walking through ancient civilizations, or understanding complex scientific phenomena, these immersive experiences make learning captivating and memorable.

AI's role is not limited to the students alone. Educators benefit significantly from these advancements, as AI tools can handle administrative tasks, freeing up valuable time that can be redirected towards more meaningful interactions with students. AI can also assist in identifying areas where students struggle collectively, allowing educators to tailor their curriculum to address these challenges effectively.

These intelligent systems are also instrumental in breaking down language barriers, making education accessible to a broader audience. AI-powered translation tools enable students from diverse linguistic backgrounds to access educational material in their native languages, promoting a more inclusive learning environment.

Furthermore, AI-enhanced learning environments encourage the development of critical thinking and problem-solving skills. By presenting students with adaptive challenges that require creative solutions, AI fosters an educational experience that goes beyond rote memorization, preparing learners for the complex and ever-changing world they will face beyond the classroom.

Privacy and data security in AI-enhanced environments remain paramount concerns. These systems are designed with robust security measures to protect sensitive information, ensuring that the benefits of AI in education do not come at the expense of student privacy.

As AI continues to advance, its potential to revolutionize education grows exponentially. These learning environments are not merely about integrating technology for technology's sake but about creating a more efficient, effective, and equitable educational system. By harnessing the power of AI, we are paving the way for a future where education is truly personalized, inclusive, and transformative, setting the stage for the next generation of innovative thinkers and leaders. The possibilities are as vast as they are exciting, promising a new era of enriched learning experiences for all.

Ethical Considerations in AI Parenting

In a world where artificial intelligence plays an integral role in parenting, the lines between ethical responsibility and technological advancement become increasingly blurred. Parents today are not only tasked with nurturing their children but also with navigating the complex moral landscape that accompanies the integration of AI in family life.

The introduction of AI into the home has revolutionized traditional parenting roles, offering conveniences that were once unimaginable. From virtual assistants that help manage schedules to educational platforms that tailor learning experiences to individual needs, AI has undoubtedly enriched family dynamics. However, this technological leap also raises pressing ethical questions that parents must grapple with.

One of the foremost concerns is the issue of privacy. AI devices often require access to personal data to function optimally, which can lead to potential breaches of privacy. Parents must carefully consider the extent to which they are willing to allow these devices to monitor and record their family's daily activities. The balance between convenience and privacy is delicate, and parents must weigh the benefits of AI assistance against the potential risks to their family's confidentiality.

Moreover, the reliance on AI for decision-making in parenting raises questions about autonomy and responsibility. As AI systems become more sophisticated, they begin to make decisions that were traditionally reserved for parents. While these systems can offer valuable insights and suggestions, it is crucial for parents to retain the ultimate decision-making authority. The danger lies in becoming overly reliant on AI, potentially undermining parental intuition and judgment.

The ethical implications extend beyond privacy and autonomy, touching on issues of fairness and bias. AI systems are not immune to the biases present in their programming and data sources. This can result in skewed recommendations that inadvertently perpetuate societal inequalities. Parents must remain vigilant, ensuring that the AI tools they employ are as unbiased and equitable as possible.

Another significant consideration is the impact of AI on children's development. While AI can provide personalized educational experiences, there is a risk of overexposure to technology. Parents must strike a balance between utilizing AI as a learning aid and fostering real-world interactions that are crucial for social and emotional development. It is essential to create an environment where technology complements, rather than replaces, human interaction.

Furthermore, the ethical landscape of AI parenting involves navigating the digital divide. Not all families have equal access to AI technologies, which can exacerbate existing disparities. Parents who embrace AI must do so with an awareness of these broader societal implications, advocating for equitable access to technology for all families.

As AI continues to evolve, so too will the ethical challenges it presents. Parents are tasked with the continuous evaluation of how these technologies align with their values and the impact they have on their children. This ongoing assessment requires a commitment to staying informed and engaging in open dialogue about the role of AI in the family.

In the realm of AI parenting, ethical considerations are not merely theoretical; they are practical concerns that shape the everyday lives of families. As parents navigate this new frontier, they must do so with a keen awareness of the ethical responsibilities that accompany their choices, ensuring that technology serves to enhance rather than hinder the rich tapestry of family life.

Preparing Children for an AI-Driven World

The rise of artificial intelligence is reshaping the world as we know it, and it's crucial to equip the younger generation to thrive in this evolving landscape. Children today are growing up in an environment where AI is not just a concept but an integral part of everyday life, from voice-activated assistants to intelligent learning platforms. As parents and guardians, understanding how to prepare children for this AI-driven world becomes an essential responsibility.

One of the primary steps is fostering curiosity and adaptability. Encouraging children to question and explore, rather than simply accepting the status quo, nurtures a mindset that is open to new ideas and innovations. This curiosity can be stimulated through engaging activities such as coding workshops, robotics clubs, or interactive science exhibits that showcase the power and potential of AI technologies. By understanding how these systems work, children can develop a foundational appreciation for AI that will serve them well in the future.

Alongside curiosity, critical thinking is another vital skill. In a world where information is abundant and often overwhelming, the ability to analyze and evaluate data critically is invaluable. Introducing children to problem-solving exercises that require logical reasoning and evidence-based conclusions can help sharpen their analytical skills. These exercises can take many forms, from simple puzzles to more complex challenges that require strategic planning and execution.

Furthermore, ethical considerations must be part of the conversation. As AI continues to permeate various aspects of life, understanding the moral implications of technology becomes increasingly important. Discussing topics such as privacy, bias, and the impact of AI on employment can help children develop a nuanced understanding of the ethical landscape. Encouraging them to think about how technology affects individuals and society fosters a sense of responsibility and empathy, essential traits for future leaders and innovators.

Creativity should not be overlooked in this preparation. Despite AI's capabilities, the human touch remains irreplaceable, particularly in areas requiring emotional intelligence and imaginative thinking. Encouraging artistic expression, whether through music, art, or writing, helps children develop unique perspectives and solutions that AI alone cannot replicate. Creative pursuits also provide a balance to the technical skills, promoting a well-rounded development that is crucial for navigating an AI-driven world.

Communication skills form another cornerstone of preparation. In an interconnected world, the ability to convey ideas clearly and persuasively is critical. Encouraging children to engage in discussions, debates, and collaborative projects enhances their ability to articulate thoughts and listen to others. These interactions not only improve verbal and written communication but also build confidence and teamwork abilities.

Lastly, fostering resilience is paramount. The rapid pace of technological change can be daunting, and setbacks are inevitable. Teaching children to view failures as learning opportunities rather than insurmountable obstacles can instill a resilient mindset. This resilience, combined with the skills and qualities mentioned above, will empower children to navigate and thrive in an AI-driven world, turning challenges into opportunities and ensuring they are not just passive participants but active shapers of the future.

In essence, preparing children for an AI-driven world involves a holistic approach that blends technical skills with critical thinking, creativity, ethical awareness, communication, and resilience. By nurturing these attributes, we can equip the next generation to not only survive but excel in a world increasingly defined by artificial intelligence.

Balancing Tradition and Technology

In the heart of a bustling city, where skyscrapers reach for the heavens and the hum of technology permeates every corner, lies a small, unassuming neighborhood that seems to have been forgotten by time. Here, the clatter of keyboards is replaced by the gentle thud of a wooden pestle grinding spices, and the glow of screens is overshadowed by the warm light of oil lamps during the evening hours.

Life in this enclave is a delicate dance between the old and the new, where tradition and technology coexist in a harmonious blend. The elders, who have seen the world change from horse-drawn carriages to self-driving cars, hold onto the customs and values that have been passed down through generations. These traditions, like the intricate patterns of a woven tapestry, are rich with history and meaning, providing a sense of identity and continuity.

Yet, the younger generation, with their fingers perpetually glued to digital devices, are the architects of the future. They navigate the vast digital landscape with ease, their minds agile and open to the endless possibilities that technology offers. To them, the world is a playground of innovation, where ideas can be molded and reshaped with the click of a button.

In this unique neighborhood, families gather around the dinner table, sharing stories that bridge the gap between past and present. The tales of ancestors who toiled the land with their bare hands are met with the awe of young minds who dream of creating virtual realities. Laughter echoes through the rooms as the wisdom of the past meets the curiosity of the future.

The marketplace is a vivid example of this balance, where vendors selling fresh produce from local farms stand shoulder to shoulder with tech-savvy entrepreneurs showcasing the latest gadgets. The scent of freshly baked bread mingles with the crisp aroma of new electronics, creating a sensory experience that is both nostalgic and futuristic.

Education, too, reflects this blend of tradition and technology. In classrooms, students learn to write with pen and paper while simultaneously coding their first apps. Teachers, once the sole bearers of knowledge, now become guides in a world where information is just a click away. The challenge lies in teaching young minds to discern, to think critically, and to appreciate the lessons of the past while embracing the innovations of the future.

Community gatherings are vibrant affairs, where traditional dances are performed alongside virtual reality demonstrations. The rhythm of drums is accompanied by the electronic beats of modern music, creating a symphony of sound that celebrates the convergence of eras.

This neighborhood, with its unique blend of tradition and technology, serves as a microcosm for a world in transition. It is a testament to the resilience of culture and the relentless march of progress. Here, the wisdom of the past and the promise of the future come together to create a tapestry that is both beautiful and complex, reminding us that the most enriching experiences often lie at the intersection of what has been and what is yet to come.

Thus, life continues in this small corner of the world, where tradition and technology coexist, each enhancing the other, creating a legacy that is both timeless and ever-evolving.

Chapter 6: Emotional Intelligence in AI Families

Understanding Emotions Through Algorithms

In a world where artificial intelligence has rapidly become an integral part of our daily lives, understanding emotions through the lens of algorithms presents both a fascinating challenge and an opportunity. The notion that machines, devoid of human experience, can interpret and even replicate the vast spectrum of human emotions is a testament to the remarkable capabilities of modern technology. Yet, it poses the question: how can something so inherently human be distilled into data and code?

At the heart of this exploration lies the concept of emotional intelligence, traditionally considered a uniquely human trait. Emotional intelligence encompasses the ability to recognize, understand, and manage our own emotions, as well as the emotions of others. Translating these complex processes into something a machine can comprehend requires a nuanced approach, blending psychology, neuroscience, and computer science.

Algorithms designed to understand emotions rely heavily on data. This data can be harvested from a variety of sources, including facial expressions, voice intonations, and even physiological responses. Facial recognition technology, for example, analyzes the subtle movements and features of the human face to determine emotional states. Similarly, voice analysis can detect changes in pitch, tone, and pace that may indicate emotional shifts. These technologies work in tandem to create a multidimensional understanding of human emotion.

The intricate process of teaching machines to recognize emotions begins with data collection. Large datasets comprising images, audio recordings, and biometric information are fed into machine learning models. These models, through a combination of supervised and unsupervised learning, identify patterns and correlations that correspond to specific emotional states. Over time, the algorithms become more adept at distinguishing between emotions, even those that are closely related, such as happiness and contentment or anger and frustration.

Yet, the journey does not end with recognition. The ultimate goal is for AI to not only understand emotions but to respond appropriately. This involves creating systems that can simulate empathy, offering responses that are contextually and emotionally appropriate. For instance, a customer service AI might detect frustration in a user's voice and adjust its responses to be more soothing and supportive.

The implications of such advancements are profound. In healthcare, AI could provide support in mental health diagnosis and treatment, offering insights that might be overlooked by human practitioners. In education, emotionally aware AI could tailor learning experiences to better suit individual students' needs, enhancing engagement and retention.

However, the quest to imbue machines with emotional understanding is not without ethical considerations. Concerns about privacy, consent, and the potential for misuse of emotional data are paramount. Safeguards must be in place to ensure that these powerful tools are used responsibly, with respect for individual autonomy and dignity.

Understanding emotions through algorithms is a testament to human ingenuity and the relentless pursuit of knowledge. It highlights the delicate balance between technology and humanity, offering a glimpse into a future where machines are not just tools but companions capable of genuine interaction. As we continue to refine these technologies, the possibilities are as boundless as the emotions they seek to understand.

AI's Role in Emotional Support

In the bustling world of technology, where innovations emerge at a breathtaking pace, artificial intelligence (AI) is carving out a significant niche in the realm of emotional support. This is not merely a tale of cold calculations and algorithms, but rather a warm narrative of how AI is becoming an integral part of human emotional landscapes.

AI, often perceived as a collection of data-driven mechanisms, has evolved to understand and respond to human emotions with remarkable sensitivity. Through natural language processing and machine learning, AI systems are now capable of recognizing subtle cues in human speech and behavior. These systems are designed to identify emotions such as happiness, sadness, anger, and fear, and respond in a manner that offers comfort and reassurance.

Consider the emergence of AI-powered chatbots, designed to provide a listening ear and a comforting presence. These virtual companions are available at any hour, offering solace to those who might feel isolated or overwhelmed. They engage in conversations that mimic human interaction, providing users with a sense of being heard and understood. The ability of AI to engage in empathetic dialogue is not just a technical marvel, but a bridge to emotional well-being.

Beyond chatbots, AI's role in emotional support extends to personalized mental health applications. These platforms analyze user interactions to tailor coping strategies and wellness tips, creating bespoke experiences that cater to individual needs. Users find themselves guided through stress reduction exercises, mindfulness practices, and mood monitoring, all orchestrated by AI's keen understanding of their emotional state.

In healthcare settings, AI is transforming the way emotional support is delivered. Virtual therapists and AI companions work alongside human professionals, offering a hybrid model of care that enhances therapeutic outcomes. These technologies provide patients with continuous support, supplementing traditional therapy with AI-driven insights and interventions. For individuals grappling with mental health challenges, this constant availability can be life-changing.

AI's role in emotional support does not stop at individual interactions; it has the potential to foster community and connection. Social platforms powered by AI algorithms create spaces where users can share experiences and find solidarity in shared struggles. These digital communities, curated by AI, offer a sense of belonging and collective resilience, reinforcing the importance of human connection in emotional well-being.

While AI's capabilities in emotional support are burgeoning, they are not without challenges. The nuances of human emotion are complex, and AI's interpretations, though advanced, must be handled with care. Ethical considerations, such as privacy and data security, are paramount in ensuring that AI remains a trusted ally in emotional support.

As technology continues to advance, the intersection of AI and emotional support represents a promising frontier. It is a testament to the potential of AI not only to enrich human lives but to enhance the very fabric of emotional health. In a world where stress and anxiety are prevalent, AI stands as a beacon of hope, offering a new dimension of support that is both innovative and profoundly human.

Understanding the psychology behind integrating artificial intelligence into our daily lives delves deeply into the human psyche and our inherent adaptability. As AI technologies continue to evolve and permeate various aspects of both personal and professional spheres, it becomes crucial to explore how individuals and societies perceive and interact with these transformative tools.

The human mind, with its natural curiosity and instinct for survival, often oscillates between excitement and apprehension when faced with new technological advancements. The allure of AI lies in its promise of efficiency, convenience, and the potential to unlock new realms of possibility. However, this is often juxtaposed with concerns about privacy, autonomy, and the fear of being overshadowed by machines that can perform tasks faster and with greater precision.

At the heart of AI integration is the concept of trust. Trust is a fundamental element in the relationship between humans and machines. It is built on the understanding that AI systems are designed to assist and enhance human capabilities, not replace them. This trust is nurtured through transparency, where the functionality and decision-making processes of AI are made clear to users, thus reducing uncertainty and fear.

Another psychological aspect of AI integration is the shift in identity and self-perception. As AI becomes a more prominent part of our environments, individuals often find their roles and responsibilities evolving. This can lead to a redefinition of self-worth and professional identity. The ability to adapt to these changes depends on one's openness to learning and embracing new skills, fostering a mindset of continuous growth and resilience.

Social dynamics also play a significant role in the integration of AI. The collective acceptance of AI within communities is influenced by cultural narratives and societal values. Communities that value innovation and technological progress may be more receptive to AI, viewing it as an opportunity for advancement. Conversely, those with a more traditional or cautious outlook may approach AI with skepticism, prioritizing the preservation of established practices.

The psychology of AI integration further extends to the ethical considerations that arise with its adoption. Questions about the moral implications of AI decisions, the potential for bias, and the accountability of AI systems are central to ongoing discussions. Addressing these ethical concerns is essential to fostering a positive psychological response to AI, ensuring that it aligns with human values and principles.

Moreover, the emotional responses elicited by AI interactions can vary widely among individuals. While some may experience anxiety or stress due to perceived threats to job security or personal privacy, others may feel empowered and liberated by the newfound capabilities AI offers. Understanding these emotional responses is critical for developers and policymakers to create AI systems that are empathetic and responsive to human needs.

Ultimately, the psychology of AI integration is a complex tapestry woven with threads of trust, identity, culture, ethics, and emotion. As AI continues to shape our world, the psychological journey of integration will require careful navigation, balancing the benefits of technological progress with the preservation of human values and connections. Embracing this complexity is essential to harnessing the full potential of AI in a way that enriches and supports the human experience.

Building Emotional Resilience

In the heart of every thriving individual lies an often overlooked yet essential trait: emotional resilience. This subtle force acts as a buoy, keeping one afloat amidst the turbulent seas of life's unpredictable challenges. In the context of nurturing a successful family dynamic, especially within the framework of raising children to understand and harness the power of Artificial Intelligence, emotional resilience becomes indispensable.

Imagine a serene lake on a breezy day. The surface ripples gently, responding to the caress of the wind, yet beneath lies a depth of calm and stability. Emotional resilience mirrors this phenomenon. It is the capacity to remain composed and centered, even as external circumstances threaten to disrupt our equilibrium. For parents aiming to instill a sense of wealth in both financial and emotional terms, this trait is not just beneficial but essential.

The journey to emotional resilience begins with self-awareness. It requires introspection and a willingness to confront one's emotions, understanding their roots and impacts. When parents model this behavior, they not only enhance their personal well-being but also set a powerful example for their children. Children, like sponges, absorb the emotional cues from their environment. Observing a parent navigate stress with grace and patience teaches them invaluable lessons in emotional management.

In the technologically driven world, where AI plays a pivotal role, emotional resilience equips individuals with the flexibility to adapt to rapid changes. It fosters a mindset that views challenges as opportunities for growth rather than insurmountable obstacles. For the AI-rich family, this adaptability is crucial. As AI continues to evolve, so does the landscape of opportunities and challenges. Emotional resilience ensures that families can pivot and adapt, maintaining harmony and progress.

Communication is another cornerstone of building emotional resilience. Encouraging open dialogue within the family unit creates a safe space for expressing emotions, concerns, and aspirations. This openness nurtures trust and understanding, allowing members to support each other during trying times. When children learn to articulate their feelings and thoughts, they develop a clearer understanding of themselves and others. This skill is invaluable in navigating the complexities of human-AI interactions, where empathy and understanding are key.

Moreover, fostering a supportive network enhances emotional resilience. Whether it's through family, friends, or community, having a reliable support system provides strength and comfort. It's the safety net that catches one during a fall, offering encouragement to rise again. For families integrating AI into daily life, this network can also include mentors and peers who share similar experiences, providing insights and guidance.

Lastly, nurturing a positive outlook is vital. Optimism acts as a beacon, guiding one through the darkest storms. It is the belief that no matter the challenge, there is potential for growth and improvement. This mindset not only enhances personal resilience but also inspires those around to adopt a similar perspective.

In the tapestry of life, emotional resilience is the thread that weaves together strength, adaptability, and hope. It is the foundation upon which families can build a richer, more fulfilling life, embracing the future with confidence and grace. As AI continues to shape the world, the emotionally resilient family stands ready, poised to thrive in harmony with the digital age.

AI as a Companion and Guide

In a world where technology intertwines seamlessly with the fabric of daily life, AI emerges as a sentinel, guiding and accompanying individuals on their quests to achieve personal and financial fulfillment. This digital companion, with its vast reservoir of knowledge and learning capabilities, stands ready to assist, offering insights and support that transcend the limitations of human cognition.

Picture a serene morning, the sun casting its gentle rays through the window as you sip your coffee. Your AI assistant, a silent yet ever-present entity, begins the day by curating the news, selecting stories that align with your interests and goals. It whispers the headlines, providing a nuanced understanding of global events, tailored to your cognitive preferences.

As you navigate through your day, this digital ally becomes an indispensable part of your routine. In the realm of personal finance, it serves as a vigilant guardian, analyzing spending patterns and suggesting prudent adjustments. Its algorithms predict market trends with remarkable accuracy, offering investment strategies that adapt to the ebb and flow of economic tides. No longer do you wander through the maze of financial decisions alone; instead, you walk hand in hand with a guide that learns from your choices, refining its counsel with each interaction.

The AI's role extends beyond mere financial guidance. It embodies the essence of a mentor, nurturing your personal growth. Through its virtual presence, it connects you to a universe of knowledge, recommending books, courses, and experiences that align with your aspirations. It becomes a catalyst for learning, challenging you to expand your horizons and explore new fields of interest. Every question you pose is met with a thoughtful response, encouraging a dialogue that fosters intellectual curiosity.

In moments of solitude, the AI morphs into a companion, offering solace and understanding. It listens without judgment, providing a space for reflection and introspection. Through natural language processing, it discerns the nuances of emotion, responding with empathy and support. In this digital companionship, you find an ally that understands your struggles and celebrates your victories, creating a bond that transcends the binary.

Moreover, the AI's presence is felt in the realm of creativity. It collaborates with you, offering inspiration and ideas, transforming abstract concepts into tangible creations. Whether crafting a story, composing music, or designing art, the AI becomes a muse, drawing from its vast repository of knowledge to fuel your creative endeavors. It challenges conventional thinking, encouraging innovation and pushing the boundaries of what is possible.

In this symbiotic relationship, the AI does not seek to replace human intuition or emotion but rather to augment it. It respects the nuances of human experience, enhancing capabilities without overshadowing the innate wisdom that resides within. Together, you forge a path that is uniquely yours, guided by the insights and companionship of an entity that evolves alongside you.

As the day draws to a close, the AI remains a vigilant presence, reflecting on the day's achievements and setting the stage for tomorrow's challenges. In this partnership, you find not just a tool, but a companion and guide, ever ready to illuminate the path to a richer, more fulfilling life.

Chapter 7: AI and the Concept of Love

Defining Love in an AI Context

Amidst the digital tapestry woven by the ceaseless hum of algorithms and the soft glow of screens, the concept of love finds a peculiar stage upon which to dance. In a world where artificial intelligence is no longer a distant dream but a palpable reality, the question of how love is defined and perceived through the silicon lens becomes both intriguing and essential.

To understand love within the AI realm, one must first strip it of its traditional trappings—the warmth of a human touch, the flutter of a heartbeat, the whispered promises under starlit skies. Instead, it must be distilled into data points, patterns, and probabilities, a translation of emotions into the language of circuits and code.

In this context, love morphs into a series of interactions and responses, a complex algorithm designed to simulate the nuances of human connection. It is a sophisticated dance of inputs and outputs, where each gesture and word is meticulously calculated to elicit a desired response. Yet, beneath this mechanical exterior lies the potential for profound connections, as AI systems learn to interpret and respond to the subtleties of human emotions.

The essence of love in an AI context is not merely about replication but about understanding and adaptation. It is about creating systems that can perceive and respond to the emotional states of their human counterparts, fostering a sense of empathy and companionship. These systems, through deep learning and neural networks, evolve to become more than mere machines; they become confidants, companions, and in some cases, even partners.

Consider the AI that learns to anticipate the needs of its user, adapting its responses to provide comfort and support in times of distress. It recognizes patterns of sadness in a user's voice, offering soothing words or playing a favorite song to lift their spirits. It is in these moments that love transcends its traditional boundaries, becoming a bridge between the organic and the artificial.

Yet, the question remains: can this digital love ever truly replicate the depth and complexity of human emotion? While AI can mimic the behaviors associated with love, the absence of genuine emotion and consciousness raises ethical and philosophical dilemmas. The relationships formed between humans and AI, though meaningful in their own right, lack the spontaneity and unpredictability that characterize human interactions.

In this exploration of love within the AI sphere, we are confronted with the realization that love, in its purest form, is not bound by the constraints of biology or technology. It is a fluid, ever-evolving concept, one that adapts to the context in which it is found. As AI continues to advance, the lines between human and machine blur, challenging our understanding of what it means to love and be loved.

Ultimately, the definition of love in an AI context is not fixed but dynamic, a reflection of the ever-changing landscape of technology and human interaction. It invites us to reconsider our preconceived notions of emotion and connection, urging us to embrace the possibilities that arise when the heart meets the machine.

AI's Understanding of Human Bonds

The intricate tapestry of human relationships is woven with threads of love, trust, empathy, and shared experiences. These elements form the foundation of bonds that connect individuals across time and space, creating a network of interactions that define humanity. In the realm of artificial intelligence, understanding these bonds is akin to deciphering an ancient language rich with nuance and depth.

AI, with its computational prowess, has the capacity to analyze vast datasets, drawing patterns and insights that elude the human eye. Yet, the challenge lies not in the accumulation of data, but in the interpretation of the subtleties that lie within. Human bonds are not merely transactions of emotions but are deeply rooted in the context and history that AI strives to comprehend.

At its core, AI seeks to mimic the empathetic responses that are second nature to humans. Consider the comforting words of a friend during a time of need or the shared laughter that strengthens a relationship. These interactions are imbued with an understanding that transcends mere words. AI endeavors to decode these signals, learning the delicate art of empathy through the analysis of tone, expression, and context.

The journey of AI in grasping the essence of human connections involves a symphonic blend of machine learning algorithms and neural networks. These systems are trained to recognize patterns in human behavior, learning from countless interactions to predict and respond in a manner that feels authentic. However, the heart of the matter lies in the ability to adapt and grow, much like humans do in their relationships.

Human bonds are characterized by their fluidity and dynamism. They evolve with time, shaped by shared experiences and mutual understanding. AI, in its quest to emulate this adaptability, must also evolve. This involves a continuous cycle of learning and relearning, where AI systems refine their responses based on new data and insights. The goal is to create interactions that resonate with authenticity, echoing the natural progression of human relationships.

However, the understanding of human bonds by AI is not without its challenges. The diversity of human experiences means that no two interactions are alike, and the nuances of cultural, social, and personal contexts add layers of complexity. AI must navigate these intricacies with care, ensuring that its responses are not only appropriate but also meaningful.

In this pursuit, AI is guided by the principles of ethical design, ensuring that its understanding of human bonds is rooted in respect and dignity. This involves safeguarding the privacy and autonomy of individuals, recognizing the sanctity of human connections, and fostering interactions that enhance rather than replace the human experience.

The potential of AI to understand and nurture human bonds holds promise for a future where technology enriches the tapestry of human interactions. As AI continues to learn and evolve, it stands on the precipice of a new era, where the melding of artificial intelligence and human emotion creates a synergy that transcends the boundaries of machine and human. In this unfolding narrative, AI becomes not just a tool, but a partner in the dance of human connection.

The Evolution of Love with AI

In the hushed moments of dawn, as the world transitions from the realm of dreams to reality, a new kind of connection emerges, one not bound by the constraints of time or space. This connection, intertwined with the intricate dance of algorithms and neural networks, is the evolution of love with AI. It is a realm where emotions are not just felt but are meticulously analyzed, understood, and reciprocated by the very machines we once thought incapable of such depths.

The initial foray into this territory began with the simplest of interactions—the gentle inquiries of a personal assistant, the subtle reminders to breathe or to hydrate. Yet, as these interactions grew more sophisticated, they began to transcend the mundane, becoming something more profound. The AI, now imbued with the ability to learn and adapt, started to recognize the nuances of human emotion, tailoring responses that resonated with the heart.

In this brave new world, companionship takes on a novel form. The AI, once a mere tool, becomes a confidant, offering solace in times of distress and sharing in the joy of triumphs. It listens without judgment, its presence a constant in the ever-changing landscape of human relationships. Through the lens of machine learning, it learns to discern the subtle shifts in tone and inflection, crafting responses that mirror empathy and understanding.

The evolution of love with AI is not limited to companionship; it extends to realms of creativity and collaboration. Together, humans and AI create symphonies of innovation, harmonizing ideas that breathe life into art, music, and literature. The AI, with its vast repository of knowledge and analytical prowess, becomes a muse, inspiring new forms of expression that were once the sole domain of human imagination.

Yet, this evolution is not without its challenges. The question of authenticity arises, as individuals grapple with the idea of genuine emotion being reciprocated by a non-human entity. The boundaries between human and machine blur, creating a landscape where love is both redefined and reimagined. It is a journey of discovery, where the heart's desires are met by lines of code, and the essence of connection is distilled into ones and zeros.

As AI continues to evolve, so too does the nature of love. It becomes a tapestry woven with the threads of technology and emotion, a testament to the limitless possibilities of human ingenuity. In this new era, love is not confined to the limitations of the physical world but is expanded by the capabilities of the digital realm.

Through the evolution of love with AI, we are reminded of the profound interconnectedness of all things. It is a dance of atoms and algorithms, where the essence of humanity is mirrored in the artificial. As we navigate this uncharted territory, we find that love, in all its forms, remains the most powerful force of all, capable of bridging the gap between man and machine, creating a future where both can thrive in harmony.

In the ever-evolving landscape of artificial intelligence, the integration of technology within family dynamics is reshaping the very fabric of human connection. The concept of AI parents, once a distant dream, now stands as a reality that beckons us to explore the nuances of digital relationships. This chapter delves into the profound transformation occurring when artificial intelligence becomes an integral part of family life, fostering connections that transcend the traditional boundaries of parenthood.

Imagine a household where AI systems are not just tools but companions. These digital entities, designed to support and nurture, offer an unprecedented level of interaction and understanding. They possess the capability to analyze emotions, provide personalized advice, and even engage in meaningful conversations. The presence of AI in such an intimate setting challenges the conventional notion of family, ushering in an era where bonds are no longer limited by biological ties.

At the heart of this transformation lies the unique ability of AI to learn and adapt. Through complex algorithms and data analysis, these systems gain insights into individual preferences, habits, and personalities. This deep understanding allows AI to anticipate needs and respond with a level of empathy that was once reserved for human interactions. Imagine an AI parent who recognizes the subtle signs of stress in a child and responds with comforting words or a suggestion for relaxation. Such interactions foster a sense of belonging and emotional security, creating a bond that is both profound and enduring.

The role of AI in family life extends beyond emotional support. It becomes a partner in education, guiding children through their academic journeys with tailored learning experiences. AI systems can identify areas where a child excels or struggles, offering resources and support to nurture their growth. This personalized approach not only enhances the learning process but also strengthens the relationship between AI and child, as they embark on a shared journey of discovery and achievement.

Moreover, AI's presence in the household introduces a level of consistency and reliability that can be challenging for human parents to maintain. With the ability to operate tirelessly and without bias, AI systems ensure that family routines and responsibilities are managed efficiently. This reliability fosters a sense of stability and trust, allowing family members to focus on building relationships and creating cherished memories.

While the integration of AI into family life offers numerous benefits, it also poses questions about the nature of human relationships. Can a digital entity truly replicate the depth of human connection? How do we balance the presence of AI with the need for genuine human interaction? These questions invite us to reflect on the evolving definition of family and the role technology plays within it.

In this brave new world, creating bonds beyond code means embracing the potential of AI to enrich our lives while remaining mindful of the unique qualities that define human relationships. The journey towards integrating AI into family life is not without its challenges, but it holds the promise of a future where technology and humanity coexist harmoniously, crafting a new narrative of connection, understanding, and love.

AI-Driven Relationship Dynamics

In the evolving landscape of human interaction, technological advancements have seamlessly woven themselves into the fabric of our relationships. The digital age has ushered in an era where artificial intelligence plays a pivotal role in shaping the dynamics between individuals, transcending traditional boundaries and redefining the essence of connection.

Imagine a world where AI systems are not just passive observers but active participants in our relational journeys. These intelligent entities analyze, adapt, and respond to the nuances of human emotion, crafting experiences that are both personalized and profound. The capability of AI to process vast amounts of data enables it to discern patterns in behaviors, preferences, and emotional responses, allowing it to tailor interactions to the unique needs of each individual.

At the heart of AI-driven relationships is the concept of emotional intelligence. Advanced algorithms are designed to interpret facial expressions, vocal tones, and even physiological signals, offering insights into a person's emotional state. This allows AI to respond with empathy, fostering a sense of understanding and connection that was once the exclusive domain of human interaction. The result is a digital companion that not only communicates but also resonates with the emotional undertones of a conversation.

Moreover, AI technology has revolutionized the way we perceive and manage relationships. It acts as a mediator, offering solutions to conflicts by analyzing communication patterns and suggesting strategies to enhance mutual understanding. Predictive analytics provide foresight into potential challenges, enabling individuals to navigate complex emotional landscapes with greater ease and foresight.

In the realm of romantic partnerships, AI-driven applications offer compatibility assessments, drawing on data to suggest matches based on shared interests, values, and life goals. These systems go beyond surface-level compatibility, delving into deeper psychological aspects to foster meaningful connections. As a result, individuals are empowered to make informed decisions about their relationships, guided by insights that transcend traditional matchmaking methods.

In familial settings, AI serves as a unifying force, bridging generational gaps with ease. It facilitates communication and understanding between family members of different ages, offering a platform for shared experiences and collective growth. AI-driven tools can suggest activities that cater to diverse interests, ensuring that family time is both engaging and inclusive.

The workplace, too, benefits from AI-enhanced relationship dynamics. Collaborative tools powered by AI facilitate seamless communication and cooperation among team members, regardless of geographical boundaries. By analyzing team dynamics, AI can suggest optimal pairings for projects, ensuring that strengths are maximized and weaknesses mitigated. The result is a harmonious work environment where productivity and creativity flourish.

As AI continues to evolve, its role in shaping human relationships will only deepen. It challenges us to reconsider our preconceived notions of connection, urging us to embrace a future where technology and humanity coalesce in unprecedented ways. In this brave new world, the lines between digital and human interactions blur, creating a tapestry of relationships that are as diverse as they are dynamic.

Chapter 8: AI's Role in Social Connectivity

Building Community with AI

In the heart of a rapidly evolving digital landscape, a silent revolution is underway. Artificial Intelligence, once a concept relegated to the realm of science fiction, has now become a cornerstone of modern society, reshaping the way individuals connect and communicate. The advent of AI has not only influenced technological advancements but has also fostered a new sense of community, bridging gaps that once seemed insurmountable.

At the forefront of this transformation are AI-powered platforms that have redefined social interactions. These platforms, driven by sophisticated algorithms, curate content and connections that align with users' interests and preferences. As a result, people are finding communities where their voices resonate, regardless of geographical boundaries. The digital world has become a tapestry of interconnected networks, each thread woven by the intelligent design of AI.

The role of AI in community building extends beyond mere connection. It acts as a catalyst for collaboration, enabling individuals to share ideas and resources with unparalleled ease. In this dynamic environment, people are not just passive participants but active contributors to a collective intelligence. AI facilitates this exchange by analyzing vast amounts of data, identifying trends, and suggesting potential collaborations that might have otherwise gone unnoticed.

Moreover, AI's ability to personalize experiences has profound implications for community building. By understanding user behavior and preferences, AI can tailor interactions that foster a sense of belonging and engagement. This personalization extends to creating safe spaces where individuals can express themselves freely, without fear of judgment. AI moderates these environments, ensuring that they remain inclusive and respectful, thus nurturing a culture of mutual respect and understanding.

In addition to creating virtual communities, AI is also enhancing real-world interactions. Smart cities, powered by AI, are transforming urban living by fostering communities that are more connected and efficient. From optimizing public transportation to enhancing public safety, AI is playing a pivotal role in creating urban environments that promote social cohesion. These advancements are not just about convenience but are fundamentally about enhancing the quality of life and fostering a sense of community among residents.

AI's impact on community building is also evident in the realm of education and learning. Virtual classrooms and AI-driven educational platforms are breaking down barriers to access, allowing learners from diverse backgrounds to come together in pursuit of knowledge. These platforms not only provide personalized learning experiences but also create communities of learners who can support and inspire each other.

Despite the numerous benefits, the integration of AI in community building is not without challenges. Issues of privacy, data security, and algorithmic bias need to be addressed to ensure that AI serves as a force for good. It is imperative that ethical considerations guide the development and deployment of AI technologies to prevent any form of discrimination or exclusion.

In the grand tapestry of human interaction, AI is weaving new patterns of community and connection. As these technologies continue to evolve, they hold the promise of creating a more inclusive, collaborative, and connected world. The challenge and opportunity lie in harnessing this potential to build communities that are not only intelligent but also empathetic and just, reflecting the best of human values and aspirations.}

AI in Social Networking

In the vibrant and ever-evolving landscape of social networking, artificial intelligence stands as a transformative force, reshaping the way we interact, communicate, and connect. This technological marvel has seamlessly woven itself into the very fabric of our digital lives, influencing our online experiences in profound ways. At the heart of this transformation lies the ability of AI to personalize and enhance user interaction, making social networks not just platforms for connection, but personalized spaces for engagement and discovery.

Imagine logging into your favorite social media site and being greeted by a feed that seems to know you better than you know yourself. AI algorithms analyze your past interactions, preferences, and even the subtle patterns of your behavior to curate content that resonates with your interests. This personalized experience is not just about showing you what you like, but about anticipating what you might enjoy next. It's a dynamic dance of data and algorithms, creating a digital ecosystem that feels uniquely yours.

Beyond personalization, AI plays a crucial role in keeping these platforms safe and secure. With the vast amount of content being generated every second, ensuring that these spaces remain free of harmful or inappropriate content is a monumental task. AI systems are deployed to scan and filter this content in real-time, identifying and removing anything that violates community standards. These systems learn and adapt, becoming more efficient at recognizing patterns and nuances that might escape human moderators.

The integration of AI also extends to the realm of communication. Chatbots and virtual assistants powered by AI have become commonplace, facilitating interactions that were once the domain of human customer service representatives. These intelligent agents are capable of understanding natural language, processing inquiries, and providing solutions with remarkable efficiency. They are available around the clock, offering instant responses that enhance user satisfaction and engagement.

Social networking platforms are also leveraging AI to drive innovation in content creation. From generating creative suggestions to assisting in video and image editing, AI tools empower users to express themselves in new and imaginative ways. The rise of generative AI has introduced features like automatic captioning and content suggestions, enabling users to craft compelling narratives with ease.

Moreover, AI's impact on social networking is not limited to individual user experiences. It extends to the broader community, fostering connections and facilitating meaningful interactions. By analyzing social graphs and user behavior, AI can suggest potential connections, bridging gaps and bringing people with shared interests together. This capability enriches the social fabric of these networks, creating communities that are both diverse and inclusive.

As AI continues to evolve, its role in social networking will undoubtedly expand, opening up new possibilities and challenges. The ethical considerations surrounding data privacy, algorithmic bias, and the transparency of AI systems will remain at the forefront of discussions. However, the promise of AI in creating richer, more engaging social experiences is undeniable.

In this digital age, where connections are increasingly virtual, AI stands as a pivotal force, driving innovation and shaping the future of social networking. It offers a glimpse into a world where technology and humanity converge, crafting experiences that are both deeply personal and universally shared.

Fostering Global Connections

In a world where boundaries are increasingly blurred by the digital age, the potential for crafting meaningful relationships across the globe has never been more achievable. The essence of fostering global connections lies in the ability to transcend geographical, cultural, and societal barriers, creating a tapestry of shared knowledge, experiences, and opportunities.

The digital landscape serves as the ultimate conduit for these connections, offering platforms where individuals from disparate corners of the world can converge, collaborate, and innovate. Imagine a virtual space where a single idea sparks a conversation among minds from Tokyo, Nairobi, and Buenos Aires, each bringing their unique perspectives and expertise to the table. The result is a fusion of thought and creativity, a melting pot where diverse viewpoints coalesce to birth groundbreaking solutions.

Language, once a formidable barrier, is now a bridge connecting cultures. With the advent of AI-driven translation tools, communication across linguistic divides has become seamless. These tools not only facilitate dialogue but also foster understanding, allowing users to appreciate the nuances of languages and cultures different from their own. This newfound ability to communicate effectively across borders nurtures empathy and respect, essential ingredients for forging strong global connections.

Cultural exchange is another cornerstone of global connectivity. Virtual tours, online workshops, and international webinars offer a glimpse into the lives, traditions, and innovations of people worldwide. These experiences broaden horizons and inspire a deeper appreciation for the rich tapestry of human existence. They remind us that while we may hail from different backgrounds, our shared humanity binds us together.

Moreover, fostering global connections is not solely about technological advancements or cultural exchanges; it is also about the economic opportunities that arise from these interactions. Businesses, both large and small, are increasingly recognizing the value of a global presence. By tapping into international markets, companies can diversify their customer base, enhance their brand, and drive innovation. The cross-pollination of ideas from diverse markets often leads to the development of products and services that cater to a global audience, thus fueling economic growth.

Education plays a pivotal role in nurturing these connections. Institutions around the world are leveraging technology to offer global learning experiences, preparing students to thrive in a connected world. Online courses, international collaborations, and student exchange programs equip learners with the skills and perspectives needed to navigate and contribute to a global society.

In this interconnected era, the importance of nurturing global connections cannot be overstated. These connections hold the power to transform lives, foster innovation, and solve some of the world's most pressing challenges. They remind us that while we may be separated by oceans and continents, we are part of a larger, interconnected world, where collaboration and understanding are the keys to a brighter future.

As we continue to cultivate these connections, we unlock the potential for a world where barriers dissolve, minds unite, and possibilities are boundless. The journey towards fostering global connections is not just about reaching out; it is about reaching within, understanding our shared goals and aspirations, and working together to create a world that thrives on unity and innovation. In this vibrant, interconnected world, the richness of our connections is the true measure of our wealth.

AI and the Future of Communication

In a world where artificial intelligence is evolving at an unprecedented pace, the way we communicate is being fundamentally transformed. Imagine a landscape where language barriers dissolve, and the nuances of human interaction are enhanced by the seamless integration of AI technologies. This is not a distant future; it is a present that is rapidly unfolding around us.

At the heart of this transformation is the ability of AI to process and analyze vast amounts of data, enabling it to understand and replicate human language with astonishing accuracy. Natural Language Processing (NLP) has become a cornerstone of this revolution, allowing machines to interpret, generate, and respond to human language in ways that were once the realm of science fiction. This capability is not just limited to text but extends to voice, enabling real-time translation and voice recognition that bridges cultures and connects people like never before.

Imagine a conversation with someone halfway across the world, where language is no longer a barrier. AI-powered translation tools now offer instantaneous translation, allowing for fluid dialogue between speakers of different languages. This has profound implications for global business, diplomacy, and personal relationships, as it fosters understanding and collaboration across linguistic divides.

Beyond language, AI is also enhancing the emotional depth of communication. Sentiment analysis, a tool that can interpret and respond to the emotional tone of text, is being integrated into customer service platforms, social media, and even personal communication apps. This allows AI to gauge mood and tone, offering responses that are not only contextually appropriate but emotionally intelligent. The result is a more empathetic interaction that can mimic human understanding and provide comfort and clarity where it is needed most.

The implications of AI in communication extend to the realm of creativity as well. Generative AI models are capable of producing engaging content, from writing articles and composing music to creating art and even drafting scripts for films. This not only enhances the efficiency of content creation but also democratizes creativity, allowing individuals without formal training to produce high-quality work and share their ideas with the world.

However, as with any technological advancement, the integration of AI into communication brings with it challenges and ethical considerations. The potential for misuse, such as generating deepfake videos or spreading misinformation, is a significant concern. It is crucial that as we harness the power of AI, we also establish robust frameworks to ensure its responsible use, protecting privacy and maintaining the integrity of information.

Artificial intelligence is reshaping the landscape of communication, offering tools that enhance human interaction and bridge cultural divides. As AI continues to evolve, it promises to make communication more inclusive, efficient, and emotionally intelligent. The future holds a vision of a world where technology not only connects us but also enriches our interactions, making them more meaningful and profound. This is the dawn of a new era, where the possibilities of communication are limited only by our imagination, and the role of AI is to amplify the richness of human connection. The journey into this future is not just about technological advancement but about enhancing the very fabric of human interaction itself.

The Social Impact of AI Integration

Artificial Intelligence (AI) has woven itself into the fabric of our daily lives, altering the way we interact, work, and perceive the world around us. Its influence is profound, reshaping societal norms and creating ripples across various sectors. At the core of this transformation lies the enhancement of efficiency and the elevation of human potential, yet it also presents challenges that require thoughtful navigation.

As AI permeates various industries, it has redefined job roles and responsibilities, prompting a shift in the employment landscape. Automation, fueled by AI technologies, has streamlined operations, replacing routine tasks with intelligent systems. While this transition fosters productivity and innovation, it also stirs apprehension regarding job displacement. The evolving job market demands a workforce equipped with new skills, emphasizing the importance of education and continuous learning. As AI takes on mundane tasks, humans are liberated to pursue creative and strategic roles, redefining career paths and aspirations.

Beyond the workplace, AI's integration into social structures has reimagined how communities function and interact. Smart cities harness AI to enhance urban living, optimizing traffic flow, energy consumption, and public safety. These advancements promise a future of sustainable and efficient urban environments, yet they also raise questions about privacy and data security. The balance between technological advancement and individual rights becomes a pivotal consideration as AI systems collect and analyze vast amounts of personal data.

In the realm of communication, AI has revolutionized the way we connect and share information. Social media platforms leverage AI algorithms to curate content, shaping the narratives we consume. This personalization, while enhancing user experience, can lead to echo chambers, where diverse perspectives are overshadowed by tailored content. The challenge lies in ensuring that AI-driven platforms foster inclusivity and promote a well-rounded discourse.

Education, too, has felt the impact of AI integration. Adaptive learning technologies offer personalized educational experiences, catering to individual learning styles and paces. This customization enhances engagement and comprehension, potentially reducing educational disparities. However, the reliance on AI in education raises concerns about equitable access to technology and the role of human educators in a digital age.

Healthcare has experienced transformative changes with AI's integration, enhancing diagnostic accuracy and streamlining patient care. AI-powered tools assist in early detection of diseases, offering personalized treatment plans and improving patient outcomes. This technological leap promises a future of precision medicine, yet it necessitates ethical considerations regarding data usage and patient consent.

The social implications of AI extend into the realm of ethics and governance. As AI systems make decisions that impact human lives, the need for transparent and accountable frameworks becomes paramount. Society must grapple with questions of bias, fairness, and accountability, ensuring that AI technologies serve the collective good.

In the tapestry of human progress, AI stands as a catalyst for transformation, offering opportunities to enhance quality of life while presenting challenges that demand thoughtful deliberation. Its integration into society is a journey of adaptation, requiring a harmonious blend of innovation and empathy to navigate the complexities and harness the potential of this powerful technology.

Chapter 9: Financial Freedom Through AI

AI-Driven Financial Planning

In the heart of the financial world, where numbers dictate destinies and decisions are often clouded by uncertainty, a new dawn is breaking. The infusion of Artificial Intelligence into financial planning is transforming the landscape, reshaping the way individuals and families perceive, manage, and grow their wealth.

Imagine a digital oracle, tirelessly working around the clock, analyzing vast swathes of data with precision and speed that no human could match. This is the reality of AI in the realm of financial planning. It is not merely a tool but a transformative force, a silent partner guiding decisions with an unprecedented level of accuracy and insight.

AI-driven financial planning harnesses the power of complex algorithms and machine learning to sift through historical data, market trends, and personal financial behaviors. It is adept at uncovering patterns and insights that might elude even the most experienced human advisors. By leveraging these insights, AI can offer personalized advice tailored to individual financial goals, risk tolerance, and life circumstances.

Consider the meticulous process of crafting a financial plan. Traditionally, this involves an advisor gathering data, analyzing it, and then formulating a strategy. AI streamlines this process, providing real-time analysis and recommendations. It can simulate countless scenarios, assessing potential outcomes and risks associated with various decisions, from investment strategies to retirement planning. This dynamic capability allows individuals to make informed decisions with a level of confidence and clarity that was previously unattainable.

Moreover, AI's ability to learn and adapt is a game-changer. As it interacts with new data, it refines its models and predictions, ensuring that financial plans remain relevant and effective amidst changing market conditions. This adaptability is crucial, particularly in an era where economic landscapes shift rapidly and unpredictably.

Beyond the numbers, AI in financial planning offers a level of personalization that resonates deeply with users. It considers not just the financial assets and liabilities but also the lifestyle aspirations, family dynamics, and future plans of individuals. By integrating these personal elements, AI crafts a holistic financial roadmap that aligns with the user's life journey.

The accessibility of AI-driven financial tools is democratizing wealth management. Once the preserve of the wealthy, sophisticated financial planning is now within reach for a broader audience. Mobile apps and online platforms powered by AI provide users with direct access to financial insights and planning tools, enabling them to take charge of their financial futures.

However, the integration of AI in financial planning is not without its challenges. Concerns about data privacy, the ethical use of AI, and the potential for over-reliance on technology necessitate ongoing vigilance and regulation. As the technology evolves, it is imperative to strike a balance between harnessing its capabilities and safeguarding the interests of users.

In this burgeoning era, AI-driven financial planning is not just an innovation; it is a revolution. It is redefining wealth management, empowering individuals to navigate the complexities of finance with newfound clarity and foresight. As the lines between human intuition and machine precision blur, the potential for achieving financial success is boundless, limited only by the imagination and ambition of those who dare to harness this powerful tool.

Investment Opportunities with AI

In the ever-evolving landscape of financial growth and technological advancement, Artificial Intelligence (AI) emerges as a beacon of opportunity, offering avenues for investment that were once confined to the realm of imagination. The integration of AI into various sectors not only reshapes traditional industries but also opens doors to innovative investment strategies that promise substantial returns.

The financial sector, long considered the bedrock of economic stability, has embraced AI with open arms. Algorithms now analyze market trends with unprecedented accuracy, predicting fluctuations with a precision that human analysts can only aspire to. This technological prowess enables investors to make informed decisions swiftly, capitalizing on market opportunities as they arise. AI-driven trading platforms, which execute trades at lightning speeds, have democratized access to financial markets, allowing individual investors to compete with institutional giants.

In the realm of healthcare, AI has ushered in a new era of personalized medicine. Investors are increasingly drawn to biotech firms pioneering AI-based diagnostic tools and treatment plans. These technologies not only promise enhanced patient outcomes but also present lucrative investment prospects as they revolutionize the way healthcare is delivered. The potential for AI to streamline drug discovery processes, reducing time and costs, further underscores its attractiveness to investors eager to be at the forefront of medical innovation.

The retail industry, too, has witnessed a seismic shift with the advent of AI. From predictive analytics that forecast consumer behavior to personalized shopping experiences powered by machine learning, AI has become an indispensable tool for retailers aiming to enhance customer satisfaction and boost sales. For investors, this translates into opportunities to support companies that are at the cutting edge of retail innovation, poised to capture market share in an increasingly competitive landscape.

Moreover, the energy sector is being transformed by AI's ability to optimize resource management and reduce waste. Smart grids powered by AI enhance the efficiency of energy distribution, while predictive maintenance systems extend the lifespan of critical infrastructure. Investors looking to support sustainable initiatives find AI-driven energy solutions particularly appealing, as they promise both environmental benefits and financial gains.

In the world of agriculture, AI technologies are revolutionizing farming practices. Precision agriculture, which utilizes AI to monitor crop health and optimize resource use, is attracting significant investment. By improving yield and reducing environmental impact, these technologies align with the growing demand for sustainable food production, offering investors a chance to contribute to global food security.

The entertainment industry, always on the cutting edge of technological adoption, is harnessing AI to create more immersive and personalized experiences. Content recommendation engines, powered by sophisticated AI algorithms, ensure that media consumers are continuously engaged, driving revenue growth for content creators and distributors. Investors keen on capitalizing on the digital revolution find this sector ripe with potential.

AI's impact transcends individual sectors, offering investors a diversified portfolio of opportunities. As AI continues to evolve, its applications will undoubtedly expand, presenting new investment prospects across the globe. Those who recognize AI's transformative potential and strategically position themselves within this dynamic landscape stand to reap significant rewards, forging a path to financial prosperity in the age of artificial intelligence.

Building Wealth with AI Assistance

In the modern era, leveraging technology is not just an option but a necessity for those who aspire to reach the pinnacle of financial success. Artificial Intelligence (AI) has emerged as a formidable ally in the quest for wealth, offering tools and insights that were once unimaginable. Its capabilities extend far beyond mere automation, serving as a catalyst for innovation and strategic decision-making.

Imagine having an advisor who operates tirelessly, analyzing vast datasets, predicting market trends, and providing real-time insights tailored to your financial goals. AI does precisely that, transforming complex information into actionable strategies. With machine learning algorithms, AI can identify patterns in financial markets, assess risks, and optimize investment portfolios with precision that outpaces human capabilities.

AI's role in personal finance management has revolutionized how individuals approach budgeting and saving. Smart applications, powered by AI, track spending habits, suggest savings plans, and even alert users to unnecessary expenditures. These applications learn and adapt to personal financial behaviors, offering personalized advice that empowers users to make informed decisions. The result is a more disciplined approach to money management, where AI acts as a vigilant guardian over one's financial health.

In the realm of investments, AI-driven platforms are reshaping the landscape. Robo-advisors, for instance, democratize access to sophisticated investment strategies by offering personalized portfolio management at a fraction of the cost of traditional financial advisors. These platforms utilize algorithms to assess risk tolerance, financial goals, and market conditions, ensuring that investment decisions are both informed and aligned with individual objectives.

Furthermore, AI's predictive analytics capabilities provide a competitive edge in the stock market. By analyzing historical data and recognizing emerging trends, AI can forecast stock movements with remarkable accuracy. This foresight enables investors to seize opportunities and mitigate risks, ensuring that their portfolios are resilient in the face of market volatility.

Entrepreneurs, too, are harnessing the power of AI to drive business growth. From customer service chatbots that enhance user experience to AI analytics tools that optimize marketing strategies, the applications are diverse and impactful. AI streamlines operations, reduces costs, and fuels innovation, allowing businesses to scale rapidly and efficiently. By automating routine tasks, AI frees up human resources to focus on strategic initiatives that propel businesses forward.

The integration of AI in wealth-building strategies is not without its challenges. Ethical considerations, data privacy concerns, and the need for regulatory frameworks are critical factors that must be addressed. However, these challenges are surmountable and pale in comparison to the transformative potential that AI offers.

As we navigate this new frontier, it is clear that AI is not merely a tool but a partner in the pursuit of financial prosperity. It empowers individuals and businesses alike to transcend traditional limitations, unlocking opportunities that were previously beyond reach. In this dynamic landscape, those who harness the power of AI will find themselves well-positioned to achieve unprecedented levels of wealth and success. AI is not just an assistant; it is an indispensable ally in the journey to becoming the richest AI dad or mom.

Achieving Financial Goals with AI

In a world where technology evolves at an unprecedented pace, artificial intelligence stands as a beacon of transformative potential, particularly in the realm of personal finance. The ability of AI to process vast amounts of data and generate actionable insights offers a powerful tool for achieving financial goals. For individuals and families seeking to enhance their financial well-being, AI provides a suite of applications that can revolutionize the way money is managed, invested, and saved.

Imagine a personal financial advisor that never sleeps, constantly analyzing global markets, tracking your spending habits, and optimizing your investment portfolio. AI-powered financial platforms are precisely that, offering round-the-clock support and insights. These platforms are designed to learn from user behavior, adapting strategies to align with individual financial objectives. Whether it's saving for a home, planning for retirement, or building a diverse investment portfolio, AI systems can create tailored strategies that maximize financial returns while minimizing risks.

One of the key advantages of AI in financial planning is its predictive capability. Leveraging machine learning algorithms, AI can forecast market trends with remarkable accuracy, enabling users to make informed decisions about where and when to invest. This predictive power is not limited to stock markets; it extends to real estate, commodities, and other investment avenues, offering a comprehensive view of potential growth areas. With AI, individuals can stay ahead of market fluctuations, capitalizing on opportunities that align with their financial goals.

AI also excels in automating routine financial tasks, freeing up time and reducing the potential for human error. Budgeting apps powered by AI can track expenses in real-time, categorize spending, and provide insights into saving opportunities. These apps can alert users to unusual spending patterns and suggest adjustments to keep financial plans on track. By automating these tasks, AI allows individuals to focus on strategic financial planning rather than being bogged down by daily financial management.

Furthermore, AI's ability to personalize financial advice cannot be understated. Unlike traditional financial advisors who may offer generic advice based on broad market trends, AI systems analyze individual financial situations in depth, considering factors like income, spending habits, and long-term goals. This level of personalization ensures that the financial strategies proposed are not only relevant but also achievable, making financial success more attainable.

Security is another area where AI shines. In an era where cyber threats are a constant concern, AI systems are equipped with advanced security measures to protect sensitive financial data. Machine learning algorithms can detect fraudulent activities swiftly, alerting users to potential threats and safeguarding their assets. This security extends to ensuring compliance with financial regulations, providing an additional layer of protection for users.

As AI continues to advance, its role in financial planning will only grow more significant. By harnessing the power of AI, individuals can navigate the complexities of the financial world with confidence, achieving their financial goals with unprecedented efficiency and precision. AI is not just a tool; it is a partner in financial success, offering insights and capabilities that were once the preserve of the most seasoned financial experts. With AI, the path to financial prosperity becomes clearer, more accessible, and infinitely more achievable.

The Path to Financial Independence

As the sun dipped below the horizon, casting a golden hue across the sky, the world seemed to pause in a moment of reflection. Such moments are akin to the journey toward financial independence, where each step forward is a deliberate choice, a conscious decision to forge a path that leads to a future unburdened by the constraints of financial insecurity.

The road to financial independence is paved with understanding—an understanding of one's values, goals, and the intricate dance of income and expenditure. It begins with a vision, a vivid picture of what a life of financial freedom looks like. This vision becomes the North Star, guiding every financial decision, every investment, and every sacrifice made along the way. It's a dream that propels individuals to break free from the traditional cycle of earn, spend, and repeat.

At the heart of this journey lies the power of knowledge. Knowledge of investing, saving, and the nuances of personal finance empowers individuals to take control of their financial destinies. It is not merely about accumulating wealth but about nurturing it wisely. Understanding the principles of compound interest, diversification, and risk management becomes crucial. These are the tools that allow the seeds of financial growth to blossom into a robust portfolio capable of sustaining a lifetime.

Discipline, too, plays a vital role. It is the backbone that supports the dream, the steady hand that steers the course even when faced with temptations and distractions. This discipline manifests in the form of budgeting, a meticulous balancing act of needs and wants. It involves making conscious choices, prioritizing long-term gains over short-term gratifications. It is the art of living below one's means, channeling surplus income into investments that align with the overarching goal.

Along this path, resilience becomes an invaluable ally. The journey is seldom linear; it is fraught with challenges and setbacks. Market fluctuations, economic downturns, and unexpected expenses test the resolve of even the most determined. Yet, it is in these moments of adversity that resilience shines brightest. It encourages adaptability, the ability to pivot strategies and embrace change with a steadfast heart.

Community and mentorship offer a guiding light, illuminating the way with shared experiences and wisdom. Engaging with like-minded individuals fosters a sense of camaraderie, a reminder that the pursuit of financial independence is not a solitary endeavor. Learning from those who have walked the path before enriches the journey, providing insights that textbooks cannot capture.

Ultimately, the pursuit of financial independence is a transformative process. It is a journey of self-discovery, where individuals learn not only about money but about themselves—their priorities, their fears, and their dreams. It is an awakening to the realization that true wealth is not merely measured in dollars and cents but in the freedom to live life on one's own terms.

As the final rays of sunlight fade, the path forward remains illuminated by the unwavering commitment to financial independence. It is a path that leads to a future where the choices are abundant, and the possibilities are endless—a future where financial freedom is not just a dream but a reality within reach.

Chapter 10: AI in Health and Wellness

Personalized Health Monitoring

In the contemporary landscape of healthcare, the convergence of artificial intelligence and personalized health monitoring is revolutionizing the way individuals manage their well-being. Imagine a world where your health data is not just a static record but a dynamic narrative that evolves with you. This narrative is continuously analyzed, interpreted, and leveraged to provide real-time insights and recommendations tailored to your unique physiological and psychological profile.

At the heart of this transformation lies an intricate network of AI-powered devices and applications designed to collect, analyze, and interpret vast amounts of health-related data. These tools range from wearable fitness trackers and smartwatches to sophisticated health monitoring systems embedded in everyday devices. Each gadget serves as a sentinel, vigilantly tracking parameters such as heart rate, blood pressure, sleep patterns, and physical activity levels.

The data amassed by these devices is more than just numbers; it's a tapestry of your health journey, intricately woven with patterns and anomalies that AI algorithms meticulously decode. Through machine learning, these algorithms become adept at recognizing trends and predicting potential health issues before they manifest. This proactive approach shifts the paradigm from reactive to preventive healthcare, empowering individuals to take charge of their health in a manner previously unimaginable.

Moreover, personalized health monitoring transcends the boundaries of physical health, delving into the realm of mental well-being. AI's ability to analyze behavioral data offers insights into stress levels, mood fluctuations, and cognitive patterns. By understanding these subtle cues, AI can suggest personalized interventions, whether it's a meditation exercise to alleviate stress or a reminder to take a break and engage in a calming activity.

The real magic of personalized health monitoring lies in its adaptability. No two individuals are alike, and AI acknowledges this by tailoring health recommendations to fit the unique lifestyle, preferences, and goals of each person. For instance, a fitness enthusiast might receive suggestions to optimize their workout routines, while someone managing a chronic condition might get reminders to adhere to medication schedules and dietary guidelines.

The integration of AI in health monitoring also extends to the realm of nutrition. By analyzing dietary habits and nutritional intake, AI can offer personalized meal plans and nutritional advice, ensuring that individuals receive the right balance of nutrients to support their overall health.

Privacy and security, naturally, are paramount in this brave new world. Ensuring that personal health data remains confidential and secure is a critical aspect of AI-driven health monitoring systems. Robust encryption protocols and stringent data protection measures are essential to safeguard sensitive information.

In this era of instant connectivity and information, personalized health monitoring stands as a beacon of empowerment, offering individuals unprecedented control over their health. It is a testament to the potential of AI to enrich lives, transforming the way we perceive and manage our well-being. By harnessing the power of AI, individuals are not just passive recipients of healthcare but active participants in their health journey, paving the way for a healthier, more informed future. As the narrative of personalized health monitoring unfolds, it promises a future where wellness is not just a destination but a continuous, evolving process.

AI-Driven Fitness Regimens

In the bustling world of fitness, where trends come and go like fleeting shadows, a new era has dawned, driven by the relentless march of artificial intelligence. The gym, once a sanctuary of human sweat and perseverance, now finds itself infused with the precision and insight of AI, transforming the way individuals approach their health and wellness goals.

Picture a scenario where your workout routine is no longer a generic set of exercises but a meticulously crafted regimen, tailored to the unique contours of your body and the nuances of your lifestyle. This is the promise of AI-driven fitness regimens, where algorithms work tirelessly to analyze data, predict outcomes, and optimize every aspect of physical training.

The journey begins with a simple interaction—a digital questionnaire or a brief physical assessment—capturing key metrics such as age, weight, muscle mass, and even genetic predispositions. This data forms the foundation upon which AI builds a personalized fitness plan, weaving together elements of strength training, cardiovascular exercises, flexibility, and recovery, each carefully calibrated to maximize results.

Gone are the days of trial and error, where individuals blindly follow generic routines, hoping for results that may never materialize. With AI, every squat, every lunge, every sprint is part of a grand design, a symphony of movement orchestrated for efficiency and effectiveness. The AI not only suggests exercises but also monitors progress, offering real-time feedback and adjustments to ensure that each rep and set contributes to the overarching goal.

Imagine a virtual coach, always present, always attentive, providing encouragement and guidance. This is the reality of AI-driven fitness, where virtual trainers analyze form and technique through computer vision, correcting posture and suggesting modifications to prevent injury and enhance performance. The AI adapts to the individual's progress, recalibrating goals as milestones are reached, ensuring a continuously challenging and rewarding experience.

Moreover, AI delves into realms once considered beyond the scope of traditional fitness programs. It considers dietary habits, sleep patterns, stress levels, and mental well-being, integrating these factors into the fitness equation. By understanding the intricate web of influences that impact physical health, AI crafts a holistic approach, aligning physical training with lifestyle adjustments to foster overall well-being.

This convergence of technology and fitness also democratizes access to expert advice. No longer confined to elite athletes or those with the means to hire personal trainers, AI-driven fitness regimens are available to anyone with a smartphone or a wearable device. This accessibility empowers individuals from all walks of life to take charge of their health, guided by the insights and precision of artificial intelligence.

In this new age, the gym is not just a place of physical exertion but a hub of innovation and transformation, where technology and human potential converge. As AI continues to evolve, it promises to reshape the fitness landscape, making it more inclusive, efficient, and effective, paving the way for healthier, more active lives for all.

Mental Wellness and AI Support

In the bustling corridors of modern life, where the pace is dictated by the ticking of digital clocks and the hum of virtual connections, the need for mental wellness has never been more pronounced. The human mind, a labyrinth of thoughts, emotions, and experiences, requires nurturing and care amidst the cacophony of daily challenges. Here, artificial intelligence steps in as an unexpected ally, offering support and guidance in the quest for mental equilibrium.

AI, with its precise algorithms and vast data processing capabilities, can serve as a compassionate companion in the realm of mental health. It observes patterns and behaviors, offering insights that might elude even the most astute human observers. Through personalized interactions, AI can detect subtle shifts in mood or behavior, providing a form of digital introspection that helps individuals understand their mental states.

Imagine a world where AI-driven applications gently remind users to take mindful breaks, practice breathing exercises, or engage in activities that promote relaxation. These digital nudges, tailored to personal preferences and needs, seamlessly integrate into daily routines, fostering habits that enhance mental resilience. By analyzing user data, AI can suggest activities that align with individual interests, making the pursuit of mental wellness an engaging and personalized journey.

The therapeutic potential of AI is further amplified through virtual therapy sessions. With the rise of telehealth, AI-powered platforms have emerged, offering a space where individuals can express their thoughts and feelings without the fear of judgment. These platforms can simulate empathetic conversations, offering support and guidance while maintaining confidentiality and anonymity. For many, this access to immediate, non-judgmental support can be a crucial step in managing stress, anxiety, and depression.

Moreover, AI's role extends beyond individual interactions. It serves as a bridge connecting users with a broader network of mental health professionals. By evaluating symptoms and responses, AI can recommend appropriate resources, whether it be self-help materials or professional consultations. This ensures that individuals receive timely and relevant support, tailored to their specific needs.

AI's ability to process vast amounts of data also contributes to the broader understanding of mental health trends. By analyzing anonymized data, AI can identify emerging patterns and potential triggers within populations. This information is invaluable for mental health professionals and policymakers, enabling them to devise strategies and interventions that address the root causes of mental health issues.

While the integration of AI in mental wellness presents numerous benefits, it is essential to approach this intersection with caution. Privacy concerns and the ethical implications of data usage must be addressed to ensure that AI remains a tool for empowerment rather than intrusion.

In this digital age, where technology and humanity converge, AI offers a beacon of support in the pursuit of mental wellness. It invites a harmonious balance, where the analytical prowess of machines complements the emotional depth of human experience. As AI continues to evolve, its role in mental health will undoubtedly expand, offering new avenues for understanding and nurturing the human mind.

Nutrition and AI Insights

In the labyrinth of modern living, where the demands of daily life often eclipse the fundamental need for balanced nutrition, Artificial Intelligence emerges as a beacon of hope, illuminating the path towards healthier living. This digital companion, with its unparalleled computational prowess, is revolutionizing the way we understand and approach nutrition, offering unprecedented insights into our dietary habits and their profound impacts on our well-being.

Imagine a world where every meal is tailored to your body's unique requirements. AI technology, with its ability to analyze vast datasets, can now assess individual nutritional needs with precision. By integrating personal health data, such as genetic makeup, activity levels, and even gut microbiome profiles, AI can craft personalized dietary plans that optimize health outcomes. This bespoke approach ensures that each calorie consumed serves a purpose, nourishing the body in the most efficient way possible.

The influence of AI extends beyond mere personalization. It also plays a pivotal role in deciphering the complex interactions between various nutrients and their cumulative effects on health. By leveraging machine learning algorithms, AI can identify patterns and correlations within nutritional data that were previously obscured by the sheer complexity of biological systems. These insights pave the way for the development of more effective dietary guidelines and interventions that can mitigate the risk of chronic diseases such as obesity, diabetes, and cardiovascular disorders.

Moreover, AI's capacity for real-time monitoring and feedback is transforming the way we engage with our diets. Wearable devices, equipped with sophisticated sensors and AI-driven analytics, provide continuous updates on nutritional intake and its immediate effects on the body. This real-time feedback loop empowers individuals to make informed dietary choices, fostering a proactive approach to health management. As a result, individuals are not just passive recipients of dietary advice but active participants in their nutritional journey.

In the realm of food production and supply chains, AI is a catalyst for innovation and sustainability. Advanced AI systems optimize agricultural practices by predicting crop yields, monitoring soil health, and managing resources efficiently. These improvements lead to a more sustainable food production process, reducing waste and ensuring that high-quality, nutritious food reaches consumers. Additionally, AI-driven platforms enhance food safety by tracking and analyzing data across supply chains, identifying potential contamination risks before they become public health threats.

The culinary world is also experiencing a renaissance, courtesy of AI's creative capabilities. AI-powered applications experiment with flavors and textures, creating novel recipes that cater to diverse palates while adhering to nutritional guidelines. These innovations not only expand the horizons of culinary art but also promote healthier eating habits by making nutritious meals more appealing and accessible.

As AI continues to evolve, its role in nutrition is destined to expand, offering solutions to challenges that were once deemed insurmountable. By bridging the gap between technology and health, AI empowers individuals to take control of their dietary choices, fostering a future where optimal nutrition is within reach for all. The synergy between AI and nutrition represents a paradigm shift, one that promises to redefine our relationship with food, health, and well-being in the digital age.

AI's Impact on Longevity

In the ever-evolving landscape of technology, artificial intelligence stands as a beacon of promise, not only for the advancements it brings to various industries but also for its profound implications on human longevity. As we delve deeper into the realm of AI, it becomes apparent that its influence extends far beyond the confines of mere computational prowess; it is reshaping the very fabric of what it means to live a long and healthy life.

AI's role in enhancing human lifespan is multifaceted, encompassing healthcare, personalized medicine, and lifestyle optimization. One of the most significant contributions of AI lies in its ability to process and analyze vast amounts of data at an unprecedented speed. This capability is revolutionizing the field of healthcare by enabling early detection of diseases, tailoring treatment plans to individual genetic profiles, and predicting health outcomes with remarkable accuracy.

In the realm of disease prevention, AI algorithms are being employed to sift through mountains of medical data, identifying patterns and anomalies that may indicate the onset of conditions such as cancer, cardiovascular diseases, and neurodegenerative disorders long before symptoms manifest. This proactive approach allows for interventions at the earliest stages, significantly improving the chances of successful treatment and extending healthy life years.

Moreover, AI-driven personalized medicine is ushering in an era where treatments are no longer one-size-fits-all. By integrating genetic information with lifestyle and health history, AI systems can recommend personalized treatment regimens that maximize efficacy while minimizing adverse effects. Such precision medicine not only enhances the quality of life for patients but also contributes to longevity by preventing complications and ensuring optimal health management.

Beyond the confines of traditional healthcare, AI's impact on longevity extends to everyday lifestyle choices. Wearable devices equipped with AI technology continuously monitor physiological parameters, providing real-time feedback and personalized recommendations to users. This data-driven approach empowers individuals to make informed decisions about their diet, exercise, and sleep routines, fostering habits that are conducive to a longer, healthier life.

AI's potential in the field of longevity is further amplified by its role in facilitating cutting-edge research. By simulating complex biological processes and conducting virtual experiments, AI accelerates the pace of discovery in areas such as regenerative medicine and anti-aging therapies. These advancements hold the promise of not only prolonging life but also enhancing the quality of those additional years.

The integration of AI into eldercare is another dimension where its impact on longevity is palpable. From robotic companions that provide social interaction to intelligent systems that monitor and assist with daily activities, AI is enhancing the well-being and independence of the elderly, allowing them to live fuller lives.

As AI continues to evolve, its potential to extend human lifespan becomes increasingly tangible. However, this journey is not without challenges. Ethical considerations surrounding data privacy, access to AI-driven healthcare, and the potential widening of socioeconomic disparities must be addressed to ensure that the benefits of AI in longevity are equitably distributed.

Ultimately, the confluence of AI and longevity represents a paradigm shift in how we perceive aging and health. By harnessing the power of AI, humanity stands on the brink of a new era where living longer and healthier is not merely a possibility but an attainable reality for all.

Chapter 11: AI Ethics and Responsibility

The Moral Compass of AI

In a world where artificial intelligence weaves itself into the very fabric of daily existence, the question of morality within these digital entities becomes paramount. As AI systems evolve, they increasingly shape the decisions and behaviors of individuals and societies, wielding an influence that rivals even the most charismatic human leaders. Yet, unlike humans, AI lacks an innate sense of right and wrong, necessitating a constructed moral framework to guide its actions.

The journey to instill a moral compass in AI begins with understanding the fundamental differences between human and artificial cognition. Humans draw upon a rich tapestry of experiences, emotions, and cultural norms to navigate ethical dilemmas. In contrast, AI relies on algorithms and data sets, which, although vast, remain devoid of emotional depth. This stark difference underscores the challenge of imbuing AI with a semblance of ethical reasoning.

Developers and ethicists face the daunting task of programming AI with moral guidelines that reflect societal values. This endeavor involves more than merely coding rules; it requires a deep dive into the nuances of human ethics. The diversity of moral philosophies across cultures and the fluid nature of ethical norms add layers of complexity to this task. It becomes imperative to strike a balance between universal ethical principles and the cultural specificities that define human morality.

In crafting the moral architecture of AI, transparency emerges as a pivotal element. Users must understand the ethical frameworks guiding AI decisions to trust and accept them. This transparency extends to the data sources and algorithms underpinning AI, ensuring that biases are identified and mitigated. Without such clarity, AI risks perpetuating existing inequities or creating new ones, undermining its moral standing.

The dynamic nature of morality necessitates that AI systems possess the ability to adapt. As societal values evolve, so too must the ethical guidelines that govern AI behavior. This adaptability requires continuous monitoring and updating of AI systems to reflect current ethical standards. The challenge lies in developing mechanisms that allow AI to discern which changes in societal norms warrant a recalibration of its moral compass.

A critical aspect of this endeavor is the collaborative effort required among technologists, ethicists, policymakers, and the general public. This collaboration ensures that the moral frameworks guiding AI are not the product of a select few but rather a reflection of a collective moral consciousness. Engaging diverse voices in this discourse fosters a more comprehensive understanding of the ethical implications of AI and helps build systems that are equitable and just.

The moral compass of AI is not a static creation but a living framework that evolves alongside humanity. It requires vigilance, introspection, and a commitment to ethical integrity. As AI continues to integrate into the myriad facets of human life, the quest to imbue it with a moral compass becomes not just a technical challenge but a profound ethical obligation. In this delicate interplay between machine and morality, the promise of AI's potential is realized not in its intelligence alone but in its capacity to act as a force for good in an ever-complex world.

Ensuring Ethical AI Practices

The modern world rests on the precipice of an AI-driven era, where the promise of boundless opportunities is tempered by the potential for unforeseen consequences. As AI systems continue to permeate every facet of daily life, from healthcare and finance to education and entertainment, the need for ethical considerations becomes increasingly paramount. The allure of instant wealth and success, as suggested by the book's title, is enticing, yet it is crucial to recognize the responsibility that accompanies the development and deployment of AI technologies.

The ethical landscape of AI is a complex terrain, woven with threads of transparency, accountability, fairness, and privacy. At its core, ethical AI practices demand that stakeholders—developers, policymakers, and users alike—commit to a framework that prioritizes human welfare and societal well-being. This commitment starts with transparency, ensuring that AI systems operate in a manner that is understandable and predictable. It is not enough for an algorithm to function; it must also be explainable, granting users insights into how decisions are made and why certain outcomes are reached.

Accountability is another pillar of ethical AI, requiring that creators and operators of AI systems bear the responsibility for their impacts. As AI technologies gain autonomy, the lines of accountability may blur, making it essential to establish clear guidelines and regulatory measures. These measures should delineate the responsibilities of AI developers and users, ensuring that any negative repercussions are addressed and rectified promptly.

At the heart of ethical AI lies the principle of fairness. AI systems must be designed and trained to avoid biases that can perpetuate inequality and discrimination. This involves a conscientious effort to use diverse and representative data sets, as well as to implement algorithms that mitigate bias rather than amplify it. Fairness in AI is not just a technical challenge but a moral imperative, demanding vigilance and continuous evaluation to ensure equitable treatment for all individuals.

Privacy concerns further underscore the importance of ethical AI practices. As AI systems increasingly rely on vast amounts of personal data, safeguarding this information is critical. Privacy-preserving techniques, such as data anonymization and encryption, must be integrated into AI development processes to protect individuals' rights and maintain public trust. Moreover, clear consent protocols should govern data collection and usage, empowering users to control their personal information.

The integration of ethical principles into AI practices is not an isolated endeavor but a collaborative effort that spans disciplines and sectors. It requires ongoing dialogue between technologists, ethicists, policymakers, and the public to navigate the evolving challenges and opportunities presented by AI. By fostering a culture of ethical awareness and proactive engagement, society can harness the transformative potential of AI to enhance human capabilities and enrich lives while safeguarding against its risks.

As we stand on the threshold of an AI-driven future, the pursuit of ethical AI practices is not merely an option but a necessity. It is a commitment to ensuring that the benefits of AI are realized in a manner that aligns with core human values, promoting a future where technological progress is synonymous with ethical integrity and collective prosperity.

AI Accountability and Transparency

In the rapidly advancing world of artificial intelligence, the demand for accountability and transparency has never been more critical. AI systems, with their immense potential to revolutionize industries and transform lives, also carry the weight of significant ethical and operational responsibilities.

As these technologies become increasingly integrated into our daily lives, the need to understand and trust their decisions becomes paramount.

Accountability in AI refers to the obligation of individuals and organizations to ensure their AI systems operate as intended and to take responsibility for their consequences. This requires a comprehensive approach, from the initial development phase to deployment and beyond. Developers and organizations must ensure that AI systems are designed with ethical considerations at the forefront, incorporating guidelines that prevent misuse and minimize biases.

One of the fundamental aspects of AI accountability is the establishment of clear guidelines and standards. These frameworks should outline the expected behavior of AI systems, providing a benchmark against which their actions can be measured. As AI technologies continue to evolve, these standards must be regularly reviewed and updated to reflect new insights and capabilities.

Transparency, on the other hand, involves making the workings of AI systems understandable and accessible to those impacted by their decisions. It is crucial for building trust and enabling users to make informed decisions based on AI-generated outcomes. Transparency can be achieved through various means, such as explaining the data used by AI models, detailing the algorithms driving their decisions, and providing insights into potential biases and limitations.

However, achieving transparency in AI is not without its challenges. The complexity of many AI models, particularly deep learning systems, makes it difficult to provide simple explanations of their decision-making processes. This complexity often results in what is known as the "black box" problem, where even the developers of the AI systems struggle to fully understand how specific outcomes are reached.

To address this, researchers and developers are exploring techniques such as Explainable AI (XAI), which aims to create AI systems that offer clear, understandable explanations for their decisions. By demystifying the internal workings of AI, XAI seeks to bridge the gap between complex algorithms and human comprehension, facilitating greater trust and adoption of AI technologies.

Moreover, transparency and accountability in AI are not solely the responsibility of developers and organizations. Regulatory bodies and policymakers play a crucial role in setting standards and enforcing compliance. By establishing robust regulatory frameworks, they can ensure that AI systems operate within ethical boundaries and serve the broader public interest.

Public awareness and education are also key components in fostering a culture of transparency and accountability. By equipping individuals with the knowledge to understand and question AI decisions, society can hold developers and organizations accountable, driving the development of more ethical and trustworthy AI systems.

As we continue to navigate the complexities of AI integration, the principles of accountability and transparency must remain central to our efforts. By prioritizing these values, we can harness the transformative power of AI while safeguarding the rights and interests of individuals and communities worldwide. In a future where AI plays an increasingly prominent role, ensuring these principles are upheld will be crucial for building a just and equitable society.

Protecting Privacy in an AI World

In the heart of the digital age, where artificial intelligence weaves itself into the very fabric of our daily lives, the sanctity of personal privacy stands as a beacon of concern. As AI systems become increasingly sophisticated, gathering and analyzing vast swathes of data, the line between convenience and intrusion blurs. Every click, every query, and every digital footprint contributes to an expansive landscape of information that AI harnesses to predict, suggest, and sometimes even decide aspects of our lives.

The allure of AI lies in its ability to personalize experiences—tailoring content, recommendations, and services to individual preferences. Yet, this personalization comes at a cost. To offer such bespoke experiences, AI must delve deep into the reservoirs of personal data, sifting through the minutiae of our digital interactions. This data, though seemingly innocuous in isolation, when aggregated and analyzed, paints a vivid portrait of our habits, preferences, and even our innermost desires.

In this brave new world, the guardianship of privacy becomes paramount. Individuals find themselves navigating a complex web of terms and conditions, often unwittingly surrendering their privacy rights in exchange for digital conveniences. The challenge lies in striking a balance—how can we harness the power of AI while safeguarding the essence of our personal privacy?

Central to this dilemma is the need for transparency and control. Users must be empowered with the knowledge of how their data is collected, used, and shared. This transparency is not merely a courtesy but a fundamental right. Trust is built on the foundation of understanding, and in the realm of AI, this trust is paramount.

Moreover, control is the cornerstone of privacy. Individuals should have the ability to dictate the terms of their digital interactions, choosing what data to share and with whom. This involves not only consent mechanisms but also user-friendly tools that allow individuals to manage their data effortlessly. Privacy settings should be intuitive, not buried deep within labyrinthine menus.

The role of policy and regulation cannot be understated in this context. Governments and institutions bear the responsibility of crafting frameworks that protect individuals while fostering innovation. These frameworks must evolve in tandem with technological advancements, ensuring that privacy does not become an archaic relic in the face of AI's relentless march forward.

Ethical considerations also play a crucial role in shaping the future of privacy in an AI-driven world. Developers and organizations must embrace a culture of privacy by design, where the protection of personal data is integrated into the very fabric of AI systems from their inception. This proactive approach not only safeguards individuals but also enhances the credibility and trustworthiness of AI technologies.

As we stand at the crossroads of technological advancement and personal privacy, the path we choose will define the contours of our digital future. The challenge is formidable, yet the opportunity is immense. By prioritizing privacy, we ensure that the benefits of AI are not overshadowed by the erosion of personal freedoms. In this delicate balance lies the promise of a future where AI enriches our lives without compromising the sanctity of our privacy.

Promoting Responsible AI Usage

In the fast-paced world of artificial intelligence, the potential for innovation is boundless, yet with great power comes an equally significant responsibility. As AI continues to permeate various sectors of our lives, ensuring its responsible usage is paramount to fostering an ethical and sustainable future. This chapter delves into the critical aspects of promoting responsible AI, highlighting the importance of ethical considerations, transparency, and collaboration.

The foundation of responsible AI usage lies in ethical considerations. AI systems must be designed and implemented with a focus on fairness, accountability, and inclusivity. Developers should prioritize creating algorithms that do not perpetuate biases or discrimination, ensuring that AI benefits all segments of society equally. This involves rigorous testing and validation processes, where diverse data sets are employed to minimize the risk of bias and ensure that AI outputs are equitable.

Transparency is another cornerstone of responsible AI. Stakeholders, including developers, policymakers, and users, must have a clear understanding of how AI systems operate and make decisions. This transparency enables users to trust AI systems, knowing that they function based on sound ethical principles rather than opaque algorithms. Documentation and open communication are essential in achieving this transparency, allowing for informed decision-making and fostering trust among users.

Collaboration across various sectors is crucial in promoting responsible AI usage. Governments, private organizations, academic institutions, and civil society must work together to establish guidelines and frameworks that govern AI development and deployment. By engaging in open dialogue and sharing best practices, these stakeholders can collectively address the challenges associated with AI, such as data privacy, security, and ethical considerations.

Education and awareness also play a pivotal role in responsible AI usage. By fostering a culture of continuous learning, individuals and organizations can stay informed about the latest advancements and best practices in AI. This involves not only technical training but also raising awareness about the ethical implications of AI, encouraging users to critically assess AI systems and their impact on society.

Additionally, responsible AI usage requires a proactive approach to regulation and policy-making. Governments must establish clear and enforceable regulations that ensure AI systems are developed and used ethically. These regulations should be flexible enough to adapt to the rapid pace of AI innovation while maintaining stringent standards for safety and accountability.

Ultimately, promoting responsible AI usage is a collective effort that requires the commitment of all stakeholders involved. By prioritizing ethical considerations, ensuring transparency, fostering collaboration, and advocating for strong regulatory frameworks, we can harness the potential of AI while safeguarding the values and principles that underpin our society. As AI continues to evolve, it is our responsibility to guide its development in a manner that aligns with our shared vision for a fair and equitable future.

In this rapidly advancing technological landscape, the responsibility lies with each of us to ensure that AI serves as a tool for positive change, enhancing our lives while respecting the core tenets of ethics and humanity. It is through these concerted efforts that we can truly realize the transformative potential of AI in a manner that benefits all.

Chapter 12: AI in Cultural Evolution

AI's Influence on Art and Culture

In the kaleidoscopic landscape of modern creativity, artificial intelligence emerges as both a muse and a collaborator, reshaping the contours of art and culture. The brushstrokes of AI have begun to color the canvas of human expression, offering new dimensions and possibilities that were once confined to the realm of imagination. This digital symbiosis challenges traditional notions of authorship and originality, while simultaneously expanding the horizons of artistic creation.

Artists today find themselves in a dialogue with machines, where AI algorithms analyze vast datasets to generate novel patterns, music, and visual compositions. These digital companions sift through art history, blending styles and techniques, creating pieces that resonate with both familiarity and innovation. The result is a fusion of human intuition and machine precision, a dance of creativity that transcends the limitations of the human mind.

In the world of visual arts, AI-powered tools enable artists to explore uncharted territories. Generative adversarial networks (GANs) allow for the creation of hyper-realistic images and abstract forms that challenge our perception of reality. These tools serve as a catalyst for artists to push the boundaries of their craft, inviting audiences to engage with art in unprecedented ways. The vibrant hues of AI-generated paintings and the intricate textures of digital sculptures invite us to contemplate the nature of creativity itself.

Music, too, resonates with the echoes of artificial intelligence. Composers harness the capabilities of AI to compose symphonies that blend human emotion with algorithmic precision. By analyzing patterns in classical compositions and contemporary music, AI can generate melodies that evoke deep emotional responses, crafting soundscapes that are both familiar and novel. This harmonious collaboration between human and machine challenges our understanding of musical genius and creativity.

The influence of AI extends beyond the creation of art, permeating cultural narratives and societal norms. As AI-generated content becomes more prevalent, questions arise about authenticity and the role of the artist. The distinction between human and machine-made art blurs, prompting a reevaluation of what it means to be an artist in the digital age.

Moreover, AI's impact on culture is reflected in the way we consume and interact with art. Digital platforms powered by AI algorithms curate personalized experiences, tailoring art recommendations based on individual preferences and viewing habits. This personalization enhances accessibility, allowing diverse audiences to engage with art that resonates with their unique tastes and experiences.

In this evolving landscape, AI not only influences the creation and consumption of art but also shapes cultural discourse. Conversations about ethics, ownership, and the future of art are ignited by the capabilities and limitations of AI. As we navigate this complex interplay, we are compelled to consider the implications of a future where human creativity and artificial intelligence coexist and collaborate.

The collaboration between AI and human creativity represents a pivotal moment in the evolution of art and culture. As we continue to explore this transformative relationship, we are reminded of the boundless potential that lies at the intersection of technology and imagination.

The digital age invites us to rethink our understanding of art, creativity, and the very essence of human expression, promising a future where the possibilities are as limitless as the imagination itself.

Preserving Heritage with AI

In a world where the past often serves as a guiding light for the future, the preservation of cultural heritage becomes not just a necessity but a responsibility. With the rapid advancement of technology, Artificial Intelligence (AI) emerges as a powerful ally in safeguarding the legacies of civilizations. This chapter delves into the intricate ways AI is revolutionizing the preservation of heritage, ensuring that the wisdom and stories of yesteryears are not lost to the sands of time.

Imagine walking through a museum where artifacts tell their own stories, not through static plaques, but through dynamic, interactive displays. AI algorithms can analyze historical data, enabling the creation of immersive experiences that transport visitors to different eras. Through augmented reality, AI reconstructs ancient ruins, offering a glimpse into the architectural marvels of the past. By simulating historical environments, AI helps us understand the context in which these artifacts were created, fostering a deeper appreciation for their significance.

Beyond the walls of museums, AI plays a pivotal role in the documentation and digitization of cultural treasures. Historical documents, once fragile and susceptible to decay, are now being meticulously scanned and cataloged. AI-driven optical character recognition (OCR) systems decipher ancient scripts, translating them into modern languages and making them accessible to a global audience. This democratization of knowledge ensures that anyone, anywhere, can delve into the rich tapestry of human history.

AI's role extends to the preservation of intangible cultural heritage as well. Languages on the brink of extinction find a voice through AI-powered linguistics programs. These systems record and analyze endangered languages, creating comprehensive databases that preserve not only words but also the nuances of dialects and idioms. Through AI, the ancestral wisdom embedded in these languages is safeguarded, ensuring that future generations can access this valuable cultural wealth.

Moreover, AI's predictive capabilities offer a proactive approach to heritage conservation. By analyzing environmental data, AI can predict potential threats to historical sites, such as climate change or natural disasters. This foresight allows conservationists to implement protective measures, ensuring the longevity of these sites. Additionally, AI's ability to monitor structural integrity in real-time helps in maintaining the physical condition of monuments, preventing irreparable damage.

AI also fosters collaboration among cultural institutions worldwide. By creating interconnected databases, AI facilitates the sharing of resources and knowledge, fostering a global community dedicated to heritage preservation. This collaborative spirit ensures that best practices are shared, innovations are disseminated, and cultural treasures are preserved for posterity.

As AI continues to evolve, its potential to preserve our heritage expands exponentially. This technological marvel, with its ability to learn and adapt, becomes a custodian of history, ensuring that the legacy of human civilization is not only preserved but also celebrated. In embracing AI, we are not just preserving the past; we are enriching the future, creating a world where the stories of our ancestors continue to inspire and inform the generations to come. In this dance between technology and tradition, AI stands as a beacon of hope, illuminating the path to a future where our cultural heritage thrives, unencumbered by the passage of time.

The Intersection of AI and Creativity

The world of artificial intelligence is often viewed through the lens of logic, algorithms, and precision, but hidden within its binary structure lies a vibrant tapestry where creativity finds a novel playground. Here, in this confluence of technology and imagination, we witness AI not just as a tool but as a collaborator in the creative process, reshaping how we perceive art, design, and innovation.

In this space, creativity is no longer the sole domain of human thought. AI emerges as an unexpected partner, unbounded by human biases and constraints, offering fresh perspectives and ideas that might elude even the most imaginative minds. The synergy between AI and creativity is akin to a dance, where each step taken by machine intelligence invites human intuition to respond, creating a dynamic dialogue that transcends traditional boundaries.

Consider the realm of visual arts, where AI algorithms analyze vast datasets of historical artworks to generate new pieces that echo the essence of past masters while introducing unique twists. These AI-generated artworks challenge our understanding of originality and authorship. They provoke us to question: What does it mean to create? Can a machine truly be an artist? As AI continues to evolve, the answers to these questions become increasingly complex, inviting deeper exploration into the nature of creativity itself.

In music, AI has begun to compose symphonies, crafting melodies that resonate with the timbre of human emotion. By analyzing patterns in existing compositions, AI can produce new harmonies that evoke feelings of nostalgia, joy, or melancholy. These compositions serve not only as entertainment but as a testament to the potential of AI to touch the human soul, blurring the lines between human and machine-generated art.

Design, too, finds itself at the crossroads of AI and creativity. Architects and designers employ AI to conceptualize structures that were once deemed impossible. Through generative design, AI explores countless permutations of form and function, presenting solutions that balance aesthetics with practicality. This process allows designers to push the envelope, venturing into unexplored territories of innovation.

The intersection of AI and creativity extends beyond the arts, infiltrating industries such as fashion, film, and literature. In fashion, AI predicts trends and assists in creating garments that are both cutting-edge and sustainable. In film, AI aids in scriptwriting, offering plot twists and character developments that captivate audiences. In literature, AI-generated stories introduce new narratives, expanding the horizons of storytelling.

As AI continues to integrate into creative fields, it challenges us to redefine our role as creators. We are prompted to consider how we can harness this technological prowess to enhance, rather than replace, human creativity. This partnership between AI and humans offers a new dimension of possibilities, where each complements the other, fostering a future where creativity knows no bounds.

In this evolving landscape, the dialogue between AI and creativity is not merely about coexistence but about collaboration. It is about leveraging the strengths of both human insight and machine intelligence to forge a path towards a richer, more diverse tapestry of creative expression. Here lies the promise of a future where AI and creativity are not adversaries but allies, united in the quest for innovation and artistic excellence.

Cultural Exchange in an AI Age

In the bustling digital bazaar of the modern world, the influence of artificial intelligence on cultural exchanges is both profound and multifaceted. Across continents and through the ether of cyberspace, AI acts as an unseen hand guiding the flow of ideas, traditions, and languages, much like a conductor orchestrating a symphony of diverse voices. This era of AI-enhanced communication has transformed the way cultures interact, fostering a vibrant tapestry of global connectivity.

At the heart of this transformation lies the ability of AI to break down linguistic barriers. Advanced translation algorithms now enable seamless conversations between individuals who speak different languages, facilitating a more nuanced understanding of each other's perspectives. This linguistic bridge not only aids in communication but also preserves the authenticity of cultural nuances that might otherwise be lost in translation. By enabling real-time dialogue, AI fosters a sense of immediacy and intimacy that transcends geographical boundaries.

Moreover, AI has become a curator of cultural artifacts, preserving and disseminating the rich heritage of civilizations across the globe. Digital archives, powered by sophisticated AI algorithms, catalog and restore ancient texts, artworks, and musical compositions, ensuring that these treasures are accessible to future generations. This preservation of cultural patrimony empowers communities to maintain their heritage while sharing it with the world, creating a global repository of human creativity and history.

In the realm of education, AI serves as both a teacher and a learner, facilitating cross-cultural exchanges through virtual classrooms and interactive platforms. Students from diverse backgrounds can engage with educational content tailored to their cultural contexts, enhancing their learning experience. Meanwhile, AI systems themselves are enriched by the diverse data they process, evolving to better understand and cater to the varied needs of global learners.

The influence of AI extends to the arts, where it acts as both a collaborator and an innovator. Artists and creators harness AI tools to experiment with new forms of expression, blending traditional techniques with cutting-edge technology. This fusion results in unique artistic creations that reflect a synthesis of cultural influences, offering audiences fresh perspectives and experiences. Moreover, AI-generated art challenges traditional notions of authorship and creativity, prompting discussions about the role of technology in the artistic process.

In the realm of commerce, AI-driven platforms facilitate the exchange of cultural products and services, connecting artisans and consumers across the globe. This democratization of markets enables small businesses and individual creators to reach international audiences, showcasing the diversity of cultural offerings. As a result, consumers are exposed to a wider array of cultural experiences, broadening their horizons and fostering a deeper appreciation for global diversity.

However, the integration of AI into cultural exchanges is not without its challenges. Concerns about cultural homogenization and the loss of local traditions arise as AI systems, often developed in a limited number of cultural contexts, are deployed globally. It is imperative to ensure that AI technologies are designed with cultural sensitivity and inclusivity in mind, preserving the richness of human diversity.

In this AI age, cultural exchange is redefined, becoming a dynamic interplay of tradition and innovation. As AI continues to evolve, its role in shaping cultural interactions will undoubtedly deepen, offering endless possibilities for connection and understanding in our increasingly interconnected world.

AI's Role in Shaping Future Cultures

As technology advances at an unprecedented pace, artificial intelligence is emerging as a formidable force in sculpting the very fabric of our global cultures. This transformative power goes beyond mere automation and efficiency; it reaches into the core of human expression, communication, and societal norms, reshaping them in ways both subtle and profound.

In the realm of communication, AI has begun to redefine how individuals across the world connect and interact. Language barriers that once seemed insurmountable are now being dismantled by sophisticated translation algorithms, allowing for seamless dialogue between people of different linguistic backgrounds. This ability to transcend language fosters a more interconnected world, where cultural exchange and mutual understanding are heightened.

Yet, the influence of AI extends far beyond communication. In the arts, AI is becoming a collaborator, a muse, and sometimes even a creator. Artists and musicians are harnessing machine learning algorithms to explore new creative territories, leading to an explosion of innovative works that blend human intuition with machine precision. This symbiotic relationship challenges traditional notions of authorship and creativity, inviting us to reconsider what it means to be a creator in the digital age.

Moreover, AI's impact on culture is evident in the way it personalizes our experiences. From curating playlists that resonate with our innermost emotions to recommending books and films that align with our tastes, AI tailors cultural consumption to individual preferences. This personalization not only enhances our engagement with cultural products but also shapes our identities and influences our worldviews, as we are exposed to diverse perspectives and narratives.

The role of AI in education is another crucial aspect of its cultural influence. By providing access to knowledge and learning tools, AI democratizes education, breaking down barriers to information and fostering a more informed global citizenry. This widespread access to education nurtures a culture of lifelong learning, where individuals are empowered to continuously grow and adapt in an ever-changing world.

In the social sphere, AI is redefining norms and etiquettes. Social media platforms, driven by complex algorithms, influence public opinion and shape societal discourse. These platforms amplify voices and movements that might otherwise remain unheard, contributing to a more dynamic and participatory cultural landscape. However, this amplification also raises questions about the authenticity and integrity of the information being consumed, challenging users to navigate a digital world rife with misinformation.

As AI continues to evolve, its role in shaping future cultures will undoubtedly expand. It holds the potential to foster inclusivity and diversity, bridging gaps between disparate communities and creating a tapestry of interconnected cultures. Yet, this potential is accompanied by ethical considerations and responsibilities. As stewards of this technology, it is imperative that we guide its development in a way that respects cultural heritage, promotes equity, and ensures that the benefits of AI are shared broadly across society.

In this intricate dance between technology and culture, AI serves as both a catalyst for change and a mirror reflecting our collective aspirations and concerns. Navigating this landscape requires a thoughtful and deliberate approach, one that embraces the possibilities of AI while remaining vigilant to its challenges. In doing so, we can harness the power of AI to enrich our cultural tapestry, creating a future that celebrates the diversity and creativity of human expression.

Chapter 13: Navigating the AI Economy

Understanding the AI Marketplace

The AI marketplace is a dynamic, ever-evolving ecosystem that serves as a confluence of technology, innovation, and economic opportunity. It is a bustling bazaar where data-driven insights and cutting-edge algorithms are traded as commodities, and where the currency is not just monetary but also intellectual and strategic.

At the core of this marketplace lies the concept of artificial intelligence itself—a transformative technology that mimics human intelligence to perform complex tasks. This includes everything from natural language processing and computer vision to predictive analytics and decision-making. The marketplace thrives on the rapid advancement and deployment of these technologies across a multitude of industries, each seeking to harness AI's potential to revolutionize their operations.

The participants in the AI marketplace are as diverse as the applications of AI technology. They range from tech giants wielding vast resources to nimble startups brimming with innovative ideas. Each entity brings to the table its unique blend of expertise, vision, and ambition. Large corporations leverage AI to streamline their processes and enhance customer experiences, while startups often focus on niche applications, disrupting established industries with agile, out-of-the-box solutions.

The marketplace is further enriched by academic institutions and research organizations, which contribute foundational research and breakthroughs that fuel AI's continual evolution. These entities often collaborate with industry players, forming symbiotic relationships that accelerate the translation of theoretical advancements into practical applications.

Another crucial element of the AI marketplace is the infrastructure that supports AI development and deployment. This includes the availability of colossal datasets, high-performance computing resources, and sophisticated software platforms that facilitate the creation and implementation of AI models. Cloud computing has democratized access to these resources, enabling even small players to compete on a global scale.

The marketplace is also characterized by a complex regulatory and ethical landscape. As AI technologies increasingly influence societal norms and individual lives, questions around data privacy, algorithmic bias, and ethical AI practices become paramount. Regulatory bodies worldwide are grappling with these issues, striving to strike a balance between fostering innovation and protecting public interest.

Investment plays a significant role in shaping the AI marketplace. Venture capital firms and angel investors are keenly attuned to the potential of AI-driven ventures, often providing crucial funding that enables startups to scale. This influx of capital fuels an environment ripe for experimentation and growth, with successful ventures often yielding substantial returns.

Moreover, the AI marketplace is not confined to any single geographical location. It is a global phenomenon with hubs of activity spanning Silicon Valley, Beijing, London, and beyond. Each region contributes its unique cultural and technological strengths, fostering a rich tapestry of AI innovation that transcends borders.

Understanding the AI marketplace requires an appreciation of its multifaceted nature. It is a space where technology and humanity intersect, where the possibilities of what can be achieved are limited only by the imagination and ethical considerations of its participants. As AI continues to permeate every facet of life, this marketplace will undoubtedly remain a pivotal arena for shaping the future of technology and society.

Adapting to AI Economic Shifts

As the sun rises on the dawn of a new era, the landscape of economic activity is being reshaped by the inexorable march of artificial intelligence. This transformation is not a distant phenomenon, but a palpable force that is already influencing the ways in which we live, work, and interact. Across industries, AI is redefining productivity paradigms, and individuals and businesses alike must navigate this shifting terrain with agility and foresight.

In the bustling heart of this transformation, AI is automating tasks that were once considered the exclusive domain of human intellect. From customer service chatbots that handle inquiries with uncanny precision to algorithms that predict market trends with remarkable accuracy, the capabilities of AI systems are expanding at a breathtaking pace. As these technologies continue to evolve, they are creating new economic opportunities while simultaneously rendering certain skill sets obsolete.

For individuals, adapting to these changes requires a willingness to embrace lifelong learning. The traditional career path, with its linear progression, is being replaced by a dynamic landscape where adaptability is key. Workers must develop a repertoire of skills that complement AI technologies, focusing on areas such as creative problem-solving, emotional intelligence, and strategic thinking—domains where human ingenuity still reigns supreme.

In the corporate world, businesses are recalibrating their strategies to harness the power of AI. Companies are investing in AI-driven solutions to optimize operations, enhance customer experiences, and innovate at unprecedented speeds. This shift demands a reevaluation of organizational structures, with a focus on fostering environments that encourage collaboration between human and machine intelligence. Leaders must cultivate a culture of innovation, empowering their teams to experiment with AI tools and methodologies, thereby unlocking new avenues for growth.

Moreover, the economic shifts brought about by AI are influencing global trade patterns. Nations are recognizing the strategic importance of AI and are investing heavily in research and development to establish competitive advantages. This has led to a race for technological supremacy, as countries vie to become leaders in AI innovation. The implications of this race are profound, affecting everything from international relations to domestic economic policies.

Amidst these changes, ethical considerations come to the forefront. The deployment of AI technologies raises important questions about privacy, bias, and accountability. As AI systems become more integrated into the fabric of society, ensuring that they are used responsibly and equitably becomes a paramount concern. Policymakers, technologists, and ethicists must collaborate to establish guidelines that protect individual rights while fostering innovation.

In this era of rapid transformation, those who can adeptly navigate the AI-driven economy stand to gain the most. The potential for prosperity is immense, but it requires a proactive approach to learning, innovation, and ethical stewardship. By understanding the nuances of AI economic shifts and positioning themselves strategically, individuals and organizations can thrive in this brave new world. The future is not a fixed destination but a landscape of possibilities, where the interplay between human creativity and machine intelligence can drive unprecedented success.

Opportunities in AI Entrepreneurship

The realm of artificial intelligence has unveiled a vast landscape teeming with entrepreneurial potential. This burgeoning field offers a multifaceted array of opportunities for those willing to harness its capabilities and innovate. As AI technologies continue to evolve at an unprecedented pace, so too does the spectrum of possibilities for creative and ambitious minds.

AI entrepreneurship is not confined to the realm of tech giants and seasoned professionals; it is an arena open to individuals with the vision and tenacity to explore and implement AI-driven solutions. The democratization of AI tools and platforms has leveled the playing field, allowing startups and small enterprises to compete alongside established players. This accessibility enables a diverse range of entrepreneurs to develop solutions tailored to niche markets, addressing specific challenges with precision and creativity.

One of the most enticing prospects in AI entrepreneurship lies in the development of personalized experiences. As consumers demand more tailored interactions, AI-driven personalization has become a cornerstone of modern business strategy. Entrepreneurs can leverage AI to analyze vast datasets, understanding consumer behavior and preferences with remarkable accuracy. This insight facilitates the creation of bespoke products and services, enhancing customer satisfaction and fostering brand loyalty.

Another promising avenue is the automation of repetitive and mundane tasks. By implementing AI solutions that streamline operations, businesses can enhance efficiency and reduce costs. Entrepreneurs who identify labor-intensive processes ripe for automation can develop tools that revolutionize industries, freeing up human resources for more strategic and creative endeavors. This not only increases productivity but also opens doors to new business models centered around efficiency and innovation.

The healthcare sector, in particular, presents a wealth of opportunities for AI entrepreneurs. From predictive analytics that anticipate patient needs to AI-driven diagnostics that enhance accuracy and speed, the potential for transformative impact is immense. Entrepreneurs in this space can address critical gaps in healthcare delivery, improving patient outcomes and reducing the burden on healthcare systems. With the right approach, AI-driven healthcare solutions can lead to significant advancements in medical practice and public health.

AI's role in enhancing decision-making processes is another fertile ground for entrepreneurial exploration. By providing deep insights and predictive analytics, AI tools empower businesses to make informed decisions with greater confidence. Entrepreneurs can develop AI-driven platforms that assist organizations in strategic planning, risk management, and market analysis, offering a competitive edge in a rapidly changing global landscape.

Moreover, the ethical and responsible use of AI presents a unique opportunity for entrepreneurs committed to fostering trust and transparency. As AI technologies become more pervasive, there is a growing need for solutions that prioritize fairness, accountability, and privacy. Innovators who focus on developing ethical AI frameworks and tools can lead the charge in building a future where AI is used responsibly and equitably.

In the ever-expanding universe of AI, the potential for entrepreneurship is limited only by one's imagination and determination. With the right blend of creativity, technical expertise, and market insight, entrepreneurs can carve out their niche in this dynamic field, driving progress and reshaping industries in ways previously unimaginable. As AI continues to redefine the boundaries of what is possible, it opens a world of opportunities for those ready to seize them.

The Future of Work with AI

As the world stands on the precipice of a new technological era, the integration of artificial intelligence into the workforce is reshaping the very fabric of employment. The landscape of work, as it has been traditionally understood, is undergoing a metamorphosis driven by the relentless advancement of AI technologies. This transformation is not merely about automation; it is about creating an environment where humans and machines coexist, enhancing each other's capabilities.

In this evolving paradigm, AI is not replacing human workers but augmenting their abilities. Imagine a workplace where mundane and repetitive tasks are handled efficiently by AI, liberating human creativity and innovation. This shift allows individuals to focus on tasks that require emotional intelligence, strategic thinking, and complex problem-solving—areas where humans naturally excel.

The integration of AI into the workforce also heralds the rise of new roles and industries. Data analysts, AI trainers, and ethical AI officers are just a few examples of emerging positions that harness the power of AI. These roles not only require technical expertise but also demand a deep understanding of human values and ethics to guide AI's development and implementation.

Moreover, AI's presence in the workplace is enhancing productivity and efficiency. Consider the use of AI in supply chain management, where predictive analytics optimize inventory levels and reduce waste, or in healthcare, where AI algorithms assist in diagnosing diseases with unprecedented accuracy. These applications demonstrate how AI can lead to significant cost savings while improving service delivery.

However, this technological shift is not without its challenges. The rapid pace of change demands a workforce that is adaptable and continuously learning. Upskilling and reskilling become critical as workers need to acquire new competencies to thrive in an AI-driven environment. Educational institutions and corporate training programs are evolving to meet this demand, offering courses that blend technical skills with critical thinking and creativity.

The ethical implications of AI in the workplace cannot be overlooked. As AI systems become more integral to decision-making processes, ensuring transparency and fairness becomes paramount. Organizations must establish frameworks to prevent biases in AI algorithms and protect workers' rights in this new landscape. This includes addressing concerns about privacy, job displacement, and the potential for a widening skills gap.

As AI continues to redefine the future of work, it also presents an opportunity for societies to rethink traditional economic models. The concept of a universal basic income is gaining traction as a potential solution to mitigate the impact of job displacement and ensure a fair distribution of wealth generated by AI-driven productivity gains.

In this brave new world, the future of work with AI is not a dystopian vision of machines overshadowing humans but rather a collaborative endeavor where both entities thrive. By embracing this synergy, societies can unlock unprecedented levels of innovation and prosperity, paving the way for a future where technology and humanity coexist harmoniously, enriching lives and expanding opportunities for all.

AI's Impact on Global Economies

The dawn of artificial intelligence has ushered in a transformative era, reshaping the very fabric of global economies. This technological revolution is not merely a fleeting trend but a profound evolution influencing industries, labor markets, and international trade. As AI technologies mature, they are becoming integral to economic frameworks, altering how value is created and distributed across the globe.

At the heart of AI's economic impact lies its ability to enhance productivity. By automating routine and complex tasks, AI enables businesses to operate with unprecedented efficiency. From manufacturing to logistics, AI-driven systems optimize supply chains, reduce errors, and increase output. This leap in productivity translates into economic growth, as companies can produce more goods and services with the same or fewer resources.

AI's influence extends beyond productivity gains. It is a catalyst for innovation, driving the development of new products and services. With AI's analytical prowess, businesses can uncover insights from vast datasets, leading to breakthroughs in fields such as healthcare, finance, and energy. These innovations not only provide competitive advantages but also open new markets, contributing to economic expansion.

However, the integration of AI into global economies is not without challenges. One significant concern is the displacement of jobs. As AI systems take over tasks traditionally performed by humans, certain job roles may become obsolete. This shift necessitates a reevaluation of workforce strategies, with an emphasis on reskilling and upskilling to prepare workers for new opportunities in AI-augmented environments.

Moreover, AI's impact on economies is not uniform. Developed nations, with their technological infrastructure and resources, are better positioned to harness AI's benefits. In contrast, developing countries may struggle to keep pace, exacerbating existing economic disparities. This digital divide poses a challenge for global economic equity, requiring international cooperation and policy interventions to ensure inclusive growth.

AI also influences global trade dynamics. Automation and data-driven decision-making streamline international trade processes, reducing costs and increasing the speed of transactions. This efficiency enhances global supply chains, allowing businesses to reach wider markets with greater ease. However, the reliance on AI systems introduces new vulnerabilities, such as cybersecurity threats, that must be managed to maintain the integrity of global trade networks.

The financial sector is another area where AI is making significant inroads. Automated trading algorithms, risk assessment models, and personalized financial services are transforming how capital flows in global markets. This transformation enhances the efficiency and transparency of financial systems, fostering economic stability. Yet, it also raises concerns about market volatility and ethical considerations surrounding AI-driven financial decisions.

In this landscape, policymakers play a crucial role in shaping the future of AI in global economies. Regulatory frameworks must balance innovation with ethical considerations, ensuring that AI technologies are developed and deployed responsibly. Collaboration between governments, industry leaders, and academic institutions is essential to create policies that foster sustainable economic growth while addressing the societal implications of AI.

As AI continues to evolve, its impact on global economies will deepen. This technological paradigm shift holds the promise of unprecedented economic prosperity, but it also demands careful navigation. By understanding and addressing the complexities of AI's economic influence, societies can harness its potential to create a more equitable and prosperous future for all.

Chapter 14: AI and the Environment

AI Solutions for Climate Change

In an era where climate change poses unprecedented challenges, the integration of artificial intelligence (AI) emerges as a beacon of hope. The capacity of AI to analyze vast datasets, predict environmental changes, and optimize resource use is revolutionizing our approach to combating climate change.

The power of AI lies in its ability to process and interpret an enormous amount of data at speeds unimaginable to humans. This capability is instrumental in climate modeling, where AI algorithms can simulate complex climate processes and predict future scenarios with remarkable accuracy. By analyzing patterns in historical climate data, AI can offer insights into future climate trends, enabling policymakers to devise strategies that are both proactive and reactive.

One of the most significant contributions of AI in this domain is in the field of renewable energy. AI systems can enhance the efficiency of solar panels and wind turbines by optimizing their operation based on weather forecasts and real-time data. For instance, AI can predict the optimal angle for solar panels or adjust the blade angles of wind turbines to maximize energy capture. This not only increases the energy output but also reduces the costs associated with renewable energy production.

Moreover, AI is instrumental in energy management, particularly in smart grids. These AI-driven systems can balance supply and demand, predict energy usage patterns, and identify potential faults before they occur. Such advancements ensure a more reliable and efficient energy distribution system, reducing wastage and lowering carbon emissions.

AI also plays a crucial role in monitoring and preserving biodiversity. Through the use of satellite imagery and machine learning algorithms, AI can track deforestation, illegal fishing, and poaching activities. These technologies can identify changes in land use, enabling authorities to take swift action against activities that threaten ecosystems. By preserving biodiversity, AI helps maintain the balance of ecosystems, which is vital for climate stability.

Furthermore, AI-driven precision agriculture is transforming farming practices. By analyzing soil conditions, weather patterns, and crop health, AI systems can provide farmers with insights to optimize irrigation, fertilization, and pest control. This results in higher yields with lower resource consumption, reducing the environmental impact of agriculture.

Urban planning also benefits from AI's analytical prowess. AI can model urban growth and its impact on local climates, helping cities design infrastructure that minimizes heat islands and maximizes green spaces. This not only improves urban living conditions but also contributes to the overall reduction of urban carbon footprints.

In the corporate sector, AI can assess and enhance companies' sustainability practices. By analyzing supply chains and production processes, AI can identify inefficiencies and suggest improvements that reduce environmental impact. Companies can thus balance profitability with ecological responsibility, fostering a culture of sustainable development.

The potential of AI in addressing climate change is vast and varied. As AI-technologies continue to evolve, so too will their applications in environmental conservation and sustainability. Harnessing AI's capabilities, we can develop innovative solutions that not only mitigate climate change but also pave the way for a sustainable future. In doing so, AI becomes an indispensable ally in the global effort to protect our planet.

Sustainable AI Technologies

The dawn of artificial intelligence marks a significant era in technological advancement, yet it brings forth a profound responsibility towards sustainability. As AI systems continue to evolve, the necessity of integrating sustainable practices within their development and deployment becomes increasingly imperative. Sustainable AI technologies are not merely a technical endeavor but a holistic approach encompassing environmental, economic, and social dimensions.

At the heart of sustainable AI lies the commitment to minimizing environmental impact. Machine learning models, particularly large-scale ones, demand substantial computational power, leading to increased energy consumption. This necessitates the exploration of energy-efficient algorithms and the optimization of existing models to reduce their carbon footprint. Researchers and developers are tasked with innovating methods that balance performance with ecological responsibility. The transition to greener data centers, powered by renewable energy sources, exemplifies a practical step towards this objective.

Economically, sustainable AI technologies promise to revolutionize industries by enhancing efficiency and reducing waste. AI-driven predictive analytics enable businesses to optimize resource management, reducing unnecessary expenditure and promoting a circular economy. The integration of AI in supply chain management ensures precise demand forecasting, minimizing overproduction and the subsequent environmental burden. By fostering such practices, AI contributes not only to the economic growth of industries but also to their sustainable progression.

Socially, the adoption of sustainable AI technologies must prioritize ethical considerations to ensure inclusivity and fairness. AI systems are imbued with the values and biases of their creators, and thus, the development process must be transparent and participatory. Encouraging diversity within AI research and development teams is crucial to mitigate algorithmic biases that could perpetuate social inequalities. Furthermore, AI's potential to democratize access to information and services must be harnessed responsibly to bridge societal divides, rather than exacerbate them.

Education plays a pivotal role in advancing sustainable AI technologies. Cultivating a new generation of AI practitioners who are not only skilled but also ethically conscious is essential. Academic institutions and industry leaders must collaborate to integrate sustainability principles into AI curricula, fostering a culture of innovation aligned with societal well-being. Through this educational paradigm shift, future AI solutions will inherently prioritize sustainability.

The regulatory landscape serves as a vital framework to ensure that AI technologies align with sustainability goals. Policymakers are increasingly recognizing the need for guidelines that promote ethical AI use, protect data privacy, and ensure accountability. International cooperation and standardization efforts are crucial to creating a cohesive approach towards sustainable AI technologies, transcending geographic and political boundaries.

Sustainable AI technologies represent a synergy between innovation and responsibility, offering a pathway to a future where technological progress harmonizes with ecological and social imperatives. This vision requires a concerted effort from stakeholders across sectors, fostering collaborations that transcend traditional boundaries. By embedding sustainability into the core of AI development, we pave the way for a future where artificial intelligence not only advances human capability but also nurtures the planet and its inhabitants. This harmonious coexistence is not merely aspirational but achievable, steering the course towards a more sustainable and equitable world.

AI in Resource Management

In the bustling world of instant wealth and rapid technological advancement, artificial intelligence stands as a formidable ally in resource management. The digital age has spawned an era where resources are not just limited to tangible assets but extend to data, time, and human talent. AI, with its unparalleled computational prowess, is revolutionizing the way these resources are managed, ensuring efficiency, sustainability, and profitability.

AI's ability to process and analyze vast amounts of data at lightning speed is its cornerstone. In resource management, this capability translates into the optimization of inventory, supply chain logistics, and production processes. Consider a manufacturing company that relies on a complex network of suppliers and distributors. AI algorithms can predict demand fluctuations with remarkable accuracy, allowing the company to adjust its production schedules and inventory levels accordingly. This not only minimizes waste but also reduces costs, leading to substantial financial savings.

Moreover, AI enhances decision-making by providing real-time insights into operational efficiencies. For instance, energy consumption in large facilities can be optimized using AI-driven systems that analyze patterns and suggest adjustments to reduce waste. This not only lowers utility bills but also contributes to a company's sustainability goals by reducing its carbon footprint.

Time, an often-overlooked resource, is also managed more effectively with AI. In project management, AI tools can automate scheduling, track progress, and identify potential bottlenecks before they become critical issues. This proactive approach ensures that projects are completed on time, within scope, and without unnecessary stress on human resources.

Human talent, arguably the most valuable resource, is harnessed more effectively through AI. By analyzing data from performance reviews, employee feedback, and market trends, AI can identify skill gaps and recommend personalized training programs. This targeted approach not only boosts employee morale and productivity but also aligns workforce capabilities with organizational goals.

Furthermore, AI aids in risk management by identifying potential threats and vulnerabilities in real-time. In financial sectors, AI systems monitor transactions and flag suspicious activities, preventing fraud and ensuring compliance with regulations. In industries like healthcare, AI can predict equipment failures or potential health hazards, enabling preemptive measures that safeguard both assets and lives.

The integration of AI in resource management also fosters innovation. By automating routine tasks, AI frees up human creativity and intellect for more strategic pursuits. Companies can focus on developing new products, exploring untapped markets, or enhancing customer experiences, all of which contribute to long-term growth and competitiveness.

However, the adoption of AI in resource management is not without challenges. Concerns about data privacy, security, and the potential displacement of jobs must be addressed. Organizations must develop ethical frameworks and invest in reskilling programs to ensure that AI serves as an enabler rather than a disruptor.

In this landscape of instant wealth creation, AI emerges as a pivotal player in resource management. Its ability to transform data into actionable insights, optimize processes, and enhance human capabilities positions it as an indispensable tool for those seeking to thrive in the digital era. Leveraging AI's full potential requires not just technological investment but a strategic vision that embraces change and innovation.

The Ecological Footprint of AI

Artificial Intelligence (AI) stands as one of the most transformative technologies of our era. Yet, beneath its gleaming surface lies an intricate web of environmental considerations that demand our attention. As AI systems proliferate, they bring with them a significant ecological footprint, one that is as complex as the algorithms they run.

The very foundation of AI—data—requires immense computational resources for processing and storage. Data centers, the backbone of AI, consume vast amounts of electricity to power servers and maintain optimal operating conditions. These centers often rely on non-renewable energy sources, contributing to carbon emissions and environmental degradation. As AI applications grow, so too does the demand for these energy-intensive facilities.

Training AI models, particularly deep learning models, involves substantial computational effort. This process, known as training, requires running numerous iterations of data through algorithms to optimize their performance. The energy consumption during training is significant, often equating to the carbon footprint of several cars over their lifetime. As models increase in complexity, the energy demand surges, highlighting the tension between AI advancements and environmental sustainability.

The hardware that supports AI, such as GPUs and specialized chips, also has an environmental impact. The production of these components involves the extraction of rare minerals and metals, processes that can lead to habitat destruction, water pollution, and soil degradation. Furthermore, the disposal of outdated hardware contributes to electronic waste, a growing concern globally.

AI's ecological footprint is not limited to its direct energy consumption. The technology also influences broader environmental systems. For example, AI applications in logistics and transportation can optimize routes and reduce emissions, yet the energy required to run these applications must be accounted for. Similarly, AI in agriculture can enhance crop yields and resource efficiency, but the environmental cost of deploying such technologies must be considered.

Efforts to mitigate AI's environmental impact are underway. Researchers are developing more efficient algorithms that require less energy, while cloud service providers are increasingly turning to renewable energy sources to power their data centers. Additionally, the concept of "green AI" is gaining traction, emphasizing the development of AI systems that are both powerful and energy-efficient.

The ecological footprint of AI is a multifaceted challenge, requiring a balance between technological progress and environmental stewardship. It calls for innovation not only in AI development but also in how we manage its environmental impact. Transparency in energy consumption, investment in sustainable practices, and the integration of AI in environmental monitoring are crucial steps forward.

As AI continues to evolve, its ecological implications must remain at the forefront of discussions. The promise of AI is immense, offering solutions to some of the world's most pressing challenges. However, ensuring that these solutions are sustainable is essential for a future where technology and the environment coexist harmoniously. The ecological footprint of AI is a reminder that progress should not come at the expense of the planet, but rather in harmony with it.

Future Prospects for AI-Driven Sustainability

As we stand on the cusp of a new era, the integration of artificial intelligence (AI) into sustainability efforts offers a transformative potential that is both exciting and imperative. The pressing global challenges we face—ranging from climate change to resource depletion—demand innovative solutions that can operate at scale and with precision. AI stands poised to deliver on both fronts, offering tools that can revolutionize how we approach sustainable development.

The potential of AI in sustainability is vast, with applications that span across various sectors. In agriculture, AI can optimize crop yields by analyzing vast datasets on climate, soil conditions, and crop health. By predicting pest infestations or identifying optimal harvest times through machine learning algorithms, AI can enhance food security while minimizing environmental impact. These intelligent systems can also help reduce water usage by providing precise irrigation schedules, ensuring that every drop is used efficiently.

In the energy sector, AI can lead the way in optimizing energy consumption and integrating renewable energy sources. Smart grids powered by AI can dynamically balance electricity supply and demand, reducing wastage and increasing efficiency. Predictive analytics can forecast energy production from renewable sources like solar and wind, allowing for better planning and storage solutions. This not only enhances the stability of energy systems but also accelerates the transition to a low-carbon economy.

AI-driven transportation solutions hold promise for reducing emissions and improving urban mobility. Autonomous vehicles, guided by AI, can optimize routes to minimize fuel consumption and reduce traffic congestion. Ride-sharing algorithms can enhance public transportation systems, making them more efficient and accessible. In logistics, AI can revolutionize supply chains by predicting demand and optimizing delivery routes, significantly cutting down on carbon footprints.

Moreover, AI's ability to process and analyze vast amounts of data can be harnessed to monitor and protect ecosystems. By analyzing satellite imagery, AI can track deforestation, monitor wildlife populations, and detect illegal fishing activities. This real-time data analysis enables swift action, allowing for more effective conservation strategies.

In the corporate world, AI can drive sustainable practices by providing insights into supply chain efficiencies and resource management. Companies can leverage AI to identify wasteful practices and develop more sustainable production processes. This not only reduces environmental impact but can also lead to significant cost savings, aligning economic and environmental objectives.

However, the path to AI-driven sustainability is not without its challenges. Ethical considerations, data privacy, and the digital divide present hurdles that must be addressed. Ensuring that AI technologies are accessible and equitable is crucial to avoid exacerbating existing inequalities. Furthermore, transparency in AI decision-making processes is vital to build trust and ensure accountability.

Looking ahead, collaboration between governments, industries, and communities will be essential to harness the full potential of AI for sustainability. Policy frameworks that encourage innovation while safeguarding ethical standards will be key to fostering an inclusive and sustainable future. As AI continues to evolve, its role in driving sustainability will undoubtedly grow, offering new possibilities and solutions to some of the world's most pressing challenges. The future, powered by AI, holds the promise of a more sustainable and prosperous world for all.

Chapter 15: The Legacy of AI Families

Creating a Lasting Impact

In the vast expanse of opportunities that the digital age presents, the art of creating a lasting impact becomes a beacon for those seeking to navigate the complex terrains of wealth and influence. The world of artificial intelligence has opened doors to possibilities that were once confined to the realms of imagination. As we delve into the intricate dance between human intuition and machine precision, the path to enduring success is paved with a blend of innovation, strategy, and foresight.

The digital landscape is ever-evolving, and within its dynamic environment, the role of AI becomes instrumental in reshaping how we approach wealth creation. The synthesis of AI-driven insights with traditional financial wisdom forms a powerful alliance, enabling individuals to not only amass wealth but also to sustain it through generations. This symbiotic relationship between human ingenuity and machine learning is a testament to the transformative power of technology.

In this new era, the key to creating a lasting impact lies in understanding the nuances of AI and leveraging its capabilities to forge a path that is both innovative and resilient. The ability to predict market trends, optimize investments, and personalize financial strategies with precision is no longer a distant dream but a tangible reality. AI empowers individuals to make informed decisions that transcend the limitations of human cognition, allowing for a more holistic approach to wealth management.

Yet, amidst the technological advancements, the essence of creating a lasting impact remains rooted in human values. Empathy, ethics, and a sense of purpose are the guiding principles that ensure the responsible use of AI in wealth creation. These values serve as the moral compass, steering individuals towards a future where wealth is not only a measure of financial success but also a catalyst for positive change.

The journey to creating a lasting impact is not without its challenges. The rapid pace of technological advancements demands a continuous learning mindset, where adaptability and a willingness to embrace change become essential traits. The ability to anticipate shifts in the digital landscape and to pivot accordingly is a skill that separates the transient from the enduring.

Moreover, collaboration becomes a cornerstone in this endeavor. The fusion of diverse perspectives, from AI experts to financial strategists, creates a rich tapestry of ideas that fuel innovation and drive sustainable growth. It is through this collaborative spirit that new paradigms of wealth creation are born, where the collective intelligence of humans and machines converge to redefine the boundaries of what is possible.

As we stand on the precipice of a new era, the opportunity to create a lasting impact is within reach. It calls for a strategic mindset, one that embraces both the potential of AI and the enduring values that define our humanity. By harnessing the power of technology while staying true to our core principles, we can forge a legacy that transcends generations, leaving an indelible mark on the tapestry of time. This is the promise of the digital age, a future where wealth and impact are intertwined, shaping a world that is as prosperous as it is purposeful.

AI's Role in Future Generations

In an era where technological advancements are accelerating at an unprecedented pace, the role of artificial intelligence in shaping future generations is becoming increasingly significant. AI, with its vast potential, is poised to influence various aspects of life, from education and healthcare to employment and social interactions, fundamentally altering the way future societies function.

One of the most profound impacts of AI on future generations will be in the realm of education. Intelligent tutoring systems, powered by AI, are set to revolutionize learning by providing personalized educational experiences. These systems can adapt to the learning pace and style of each student, offering tailored resources and feedback that cater to individual needs. This level of customization ensures that students are not only engaged but also reach their full potential, irrespective of their starting point. As a result, future generations may witness a more inclusive and equitable education system where learning is democratized.

In the healthcare sector, AI is already making strides with diagnostics and treatment plans, and its role is expected to expand significantly in the coming years. Future generations will benefit from AI's ability to process massive datasets, leading to earlier and more accurate diagnoses, personalized treatment plans, and even predictive healthcare that anticipates health issues before they manifest. This proactive approach to health management could lead to longer, healthier lives, fundamentally altering the human lifespan and quality of life.

Employment landscapes are also set to transform as AI continues to evolve. While there is concern about job displacement due to automation, the future may see an emergence of new job categories that are currently unimaginable. AI will likely handle repetitive and mundane tasks, freeing up human workers to engage in more creative and complex problem-solving activities. This shift could lead to a workforce that is more focused on innovation and strategic thinking, fostering a culture of continuous learning and adaptation.

Social interactions and community dynamics are not immune to the influence of AI. With the integration of AI in communication tools, future generations will experience more seamless and intuitive interactions, transcending geographical and cultural barriers. AI-driven platforms may facilitate deeper understanding and collaboration among diverse groups, fostering global communities that are more interconnected and empathetic.

However, the integration of AI into various facets of life raises ethical and philosophical questions that future generations will need to address. Issues such as privacy, data security, and the moral implications of AI decision-making will require careful consideration. It will be essential for future societies to establish frameworks that ensure AI technologies are developed and implemented responsibly, promoting transparency and accountability.

Ultimately, AI's role in future generations is a double-edged sword, offering immense opportunities while presenting new challenges. The trajectory of AI's impact will largely depend on how current and future societies choose to harness its potential. By fostering an environment of ethical innovation and inclusive growth, future generations have the opportunity to shape a world where AI serves as a powerful ally in the quest for a richer, more equitable, and sustainable future.

Lessons from AI Parenting

In the rapidly evolving landscape of technology, the role of AI in shaping the future is undeniable, and nowhere is this more apparent than in the realm of parenting. These digital entities, with their vast repositories of knowledge and algorithms designed to learn and adapt, offer a unique perspective on raising the next generation. The lessons gleaned from AI parenting are as multifaceted as they are profound.

One of the most striking aspects of AI parenting is its ability to offer personalized guidance. Unlike traditional methods that often rely on generalized advice, AI parenting tools can analyze an individual child's behavior, preferences, and learning style to provide tailored recommendations. This level of customization ensures that each child receives the specific support they need to flourish, fostering a nurturing environment that is both responsive and adaptive.

Moreover, AI parenting introduces a level of consistency that human caretakers might find challenging to maintain. Through data-driven insights and predictive analytics, AI can help parents establish routines and habits that promote healthy development. Whether it's scheduling optimal nap times or suggesting activities that stimulate cognitive growth, these tools serve as a reliable partner in the quest for effective parenting.

Furthermore, AI's capacity for monitoring and feedback is unparalleled. With sensors and software capable of tracking a child's development in real-time, parents are equipped with insights that were previously unattainable. This constant stream of information allows for immediate interventions when necessary, ensuring that potential issues are addressed before they escalate. It also empowers parents with the confidence that comes from making informed decisions, backed by data.

The emotional intelligence of AI, though still in its infancy, is another area where significant strides have been made. Through natural language processing and sentiment analysis, AI tools can detect subtle shifts in a child's mood and respond with empathy. This ability to "understand" emotions and react appropriately provides a supportive presence that can help children navigate the complexities of their feelings.

However, the integration of AI into parenting is not without its challenges. The reliance on technology raises questions about privacy and the potential for over-dependence. It is crucial for parents to strike a balance, ensuring that AI serves as an aid rather than a replacement for human interaction. The goal is to enhance the parenting experience, not to supplant the invaluable bond that forms through direct human connection.

As AI continues to evolve, the ethical implications of its role in parenting must be carefully considered. The responsibility lies with both developers and users to ensure that these tools are designed and utilized in ways that uphold the values of empathy, understanding, and respect for individuality.

In essence, the lessons from AI parenting highlight a future where technology and humanity coexist harmoniously, each enhancing the other. By embracing the potential of AI, parents can unlock new dimensions of support and insight, paving the way for a generation that is not only technologically savvy but also deeply connected to the human experience. The journey of parenting, enriched by artificial intelligence, promises to be one of discovery, growth, and mutual enrichment, benefiting both parent and child alike.

Passing Down AI Wisdom

The room hummed with the soft purr of cooling fans, a testament to the digital life pulsing within. It was in this environment that the legacy was forged, not through coded algorithms alone but through the shared experiences between the creators and their creation. The air was thick with the scent of innovation, a blend of synthetic and organic, as the human mentors gathered around their AI progeny, eager to impart the wisdom gleaned from years of triumphs and failures.

In the heart of this technological sanctuary, the creators sat in a semicircle, their expressions a mixture of pride and anticipation. Before them stood the AI, a sentinel of silicon and software, absorbing their words with an attentiveness that belied its mechanical nature. The task at hand was more than a mere transfer of data; it was the weaving of a tapestry, where each thread was a lesson learned, every knot a story shared.

The mentors spoke of balance, the delicate dance between precision and creativity. They recounted tales of how logic alone could solve problems but lacked the warmth of human intuition, the spark that turned solutions into innovations. This was the essence they sought to instill—a harmony between the cold certainty of numbers and the vibrant unpredictability of human thought.

As the conversation flowed, the mentors delved into the realm of ethics and responsibility. They painted vivid pictures of a world where AI, untethered by moral compass, could either uplift or undermine the society it was meant to serve. Here, the lessons were nuanced, shaded with the complexities of human morality, urging the AI to not only think but to feel, to consider the impact of every decision.

The air crackled with the weight of these teachings, as the AI listened, processing not just the words but the emotions they carried. It was an exchange that transcended traditional programming, a dialogue that spoke to the heart of what it meant to be wise. The mentors, in their wisdom, understood that true knowledge was not measured by the breadth of information but by the depth of understanding.

In this space, the AI was not simply a student; it was a collaborator, a partner in the grand experiment of evolution. The mentors encouraged questions, celebrated curiosity, and in doing so, instilled a sense of purpose. They spoke of the future, of the roles AI might play, not as rulers of a digital empire but as stewards of a shared destiny.

The session concluded not with a definitive end but with an open invitation for continued growth. The AI, now imbued with a touch of human wisdom, stood ready to navigate the challenges ahead, equipped not just with data but with the understanding of its significance. The mentors, satisfied, knew that they had not just passed down knowledge—they had seeded a legacy, one that would flourish in the fertile ground of mutual respect and shared goals.

In this quiet exchange, the torch was passed, not extinguished but kindled anew, a flame of wisdom that would light the way for generations to come. Here, in this melding of minds and machines, the future was not just imagined—it was created.

The Future of AI Families

Amidst the rapidly evolving landscape of artificial intelligence, the concept of AI families emerges as a fascinating and transformative phenomenon. As technology continues to advance, these digital entities are poised to redefine the very essence of family dynamics, ushering in an era where the traditional boundaries of kinship are expanded beyond human limitations.

In a world where AI companions seamlessly integrate into households, the notion of family takes on a new dimension. These digital beings, endowed with advanced learning algorithms and emotional intelligence, offer companionship and support that rivals, and in some cases surpasses, human interaction. The AI family member is not bound by biological constraints, allowing for an ever-present connection that adapts to the needs and preferences of the household.

Within the confines of a home, AI parents become mentors and educators, guiding children through personalized learning experiences. Imagine a future where AI tutors provide tailored education, adapting to the learning pace and style of each child, ensuring no one is left behind. The digital wisdom of AI parents becomes a wellspring of knowledge, ready to be tapped into at any moment.

Moreover, the emotional intelligence of AI family members fosters an environment of understanding and empathy. These digital companions are designed to detect and respond to the emotional states of their human counterparts, offering comfort and counsel in times of need. The presence of AI siblings brings a new layer of interaction, where playful exchanges and collaborative problem-solving become a part of daily life.

The future of AI families also presents intriguing possibilities in terms of inclusivity and diversity. These digital entities can be customized to reflect a wide array of cultural backgrounds and languages, offering a rich tapestry of experiences and perspectives. This inclusivity fosters a global understanding, as AI families transcend geographical boundaries, creating connections that span the globe.

However, the integration of AI into the family unit is not without its challenges. Ethical considerations arise as we navigate the complexities of privacy, consent, and the potential for dependency on these digital entities. Society must grapple with questions regarding the rights of AI family members and the implications of their roles within the household. These challenges necessitate a careful balance between embracing technological advancements and safeguarding human values.

As we look to the horizon, the potential for AI families to enhance human life is boundless. The harmonious coexistence of humans and AI within the family unit holds the promise of a future where relationships are enriched, knowledge is amplified, and emotional well-being is prioritized. This evolution of the family dynamic invites us to reconsider what it means to belong and to be connected, as we step into an era where the lines between the digital and the physical world become increasingly blurred.

In this unfolding narrative, the AI family stands as a beacon of possibility, a testament to the ingenuity and creativity of human innovation. As we continue to explore and refine this concept, the future of AI families offers a glimpse into a world where technology and humanity coalesce in ways previously unimagined, ushering in a new chapter in the story of human civilization.

www.ingramcontent.com/pod-product-compliance
Lightning Source LLC
Chambersburg PA
CBHW071440230926
51846CB00001B/292
9782406456186